forever

How To

*M*arry

The

Right Guy

Over thirty years of research on

successful love and marriage around the world

has taught us many things,

but, first and foremost among them is this --

the number one prerequisite to a successful marriage

is marrying the right guy in the first place.

HOW TO

*M*ARRY

THE

RIGHT GUY

BY THE AUTHORS OF
*BUILDING A LOVE THAT LASTS:
THE SEVEN SURPRISING SECRETS OF SUCCESSFUL MARRIAGE*

Best Relationship and Marriage Book
Mom's Choice ~ Nautilus Book ~ INDIE Book
Award Winner

Dr. Charles D. Schmitz

*Dean and Professor Emeritus of Counseling and Family Therapy
University of Missouri-St. Louis*

Dr. Elizabeth A. Schmitz

President, Successful Marriage Reflections, LLC

"America's #1 Love and Marriage Experts"

Briarcliff

Publishing

Published by Briarcliff Publishing

Original book cover by Sandy Morris
Photographs by Pat Romano and August Jennewein

Library of Congress Cataloging-in-Publication Data.
Schmitz, Charles D., 1946-
    How to marry the right guy /
    by Dr. Charles D. Schmitz, Dr. Elizabeth A. Schmitz.
    pages cm.
    ISBN 978-0-9800554-5-0 (alk. paper)
    1. Marriage. 2. Love. 3. Man-woman relationships.
    I. Schmitz, Elizabeth A., 1948- II. Title.

    HQ519.S362 2014
    306.81--dc23
                        2013028852

Summary: "Based upon thirty years of research in the USA, 48 countries, and on all seven continents, marrying the right guy is a proven prerequisite for a successful marriage. Research findings discussed are how to: be ready for love, find the right guy, ask the critical questions, and sustain a relationship" – Provided by publisher.

Printed by Walsworth Publishing Company

PRINTED IN THE UNITED STATES OF AMERICA
10 9 8 7 6 5 4 3 2 1
First Edition

W

E DEDICATE THIS BOOK

to the thousands of women who graciously shared with us their stories about how they found the love of their life and to our own story of finding true love that continues to blossom in its passion, love and friendship after almost 50 years.

About the Authors

*I*N ADDITION TO BEING AMERICA'S NUMBER 1 Love and Marriage Experts and an Internet sensation, Dr. Charles and Dr. Elizabeth Schmitz are the authors of the bestselling, multiple award-winning book, Building a Love that Lasts, as well as the award-winning classic, Golden Anniversaries. They have appeared on ABC, CBS, NBC, FOX, NPR, WGN, TBN, two PBS Specials, and radio stations worldwide. Their work is featured on Examiner.com, Fabulously40.com, SimpleThingsMatter.com, SelfGrowth.com, RelateSpace.com and YourTango.com.

With more than 30 years of research experience on relationships and successful marriage on all seven continents of the world, as well as their own 47-year marriage, the Doctors know what makes relationships, love and marriage work. Their distinguished careers include over 65 awards, 650 books, articles and manuscripts, and 1000 speeches.

Dr. Charles D. Schmitz was a highly successful faculty member and administrator in higher education for over 40 years. He received his Ph.D. from the University of Missouri-Columbia. Currently he is Dean Emeritus of the College of Education and Professor Emeritus of Counseling and Family Therapy at the University of Missouri-St. Louis.

Dr. Elizabeth A. Schmitz is president of Successful Marriage Reflections, LLC. She was an award-winning educator for nearly 40 years, and has lectured extensively in college courses in the areas of counseling and leadership. Having received her doctoral degree from the University of Missouri-Columbia, she is an acclaimed researcher and author.

Contents

About the Research

*F*OR MORE THAN 30 YEARS, Dr. Charles Schmitz and Dr. Elizabeth Schmitz have traveled to the ends of the world and back in their quest to find out what all successful marriages have in common. Recently back from Antarctica, the most isolated continent on the planet, the Doctors became the first marriage researchers to have interviewed successfully married couples in all 50 states of the USA, 48 countries and all seven continents of the world—people of different ages, ethnicities and faiths.

Unlike other relationship experts and authors, the Doctors have taken a fresh and positive approach in determining that the best way to understand successful relationships is to study successful relationships throughout the world. They know that you can't understand success by studying failure—you learn about success by studying success. Success is not the absence of failure but rather the joy and beauty of happiness. The Doctors focus on what's right about relationships and marriage, rather than what's wrong.

With this positive approach, the natural question the Doctors had for the thousands of happily married women they interviewed throughout the world was, "How did you find the right guy when so many other women fell in love and married the wrong guy?" It became blatantly obvious that these successfully married women all had similar stories using the same critical elements in their selection process.

After analyzing their stories, the Doctors discovered 33 indicators that predict if a woman will have a successful marriage with the man she is thinking about marrying. These 33 factors are the basis for the Marry the Right Guy Quiz and the foundation for the information provided throughout this book to help women make great decisions about who to marry so they can live happily ever after.

MARRY THE RIGHT GUY QUIZ

So you think you have finally found Mr. Right. If so, you should be able to pass this simple test, based upon more than 30 years of research with successful couples in 48 countries on all seven continents of the world. Please review the 33 questions below and record your answer to each as True or False.

CIRCLE TRUE OR FALSE

TRUE OR FALSE 1. I often think about or dwell on a past relationship.

TRUE OR FALSE 2. I am physically and emotionally in a healthy state most of the time.

TRUE OR FALSE 3. I can accept the guy I love as he is today.

TRUE OR FALSE 4. My guy occasionally tells lies to other people.

TRUE OR FALSE 5. The same things that matter most to me matter most to him.

TRUE OR FALSE 6. My beliefs (core values) are compatible with his.

TRUE OR FALSE 7. My best friend is someone other than the guy I love.

TRUE OR FALSE 8. There are times when I am not sure he really loves me.

TRUE OR FALSE 9. Our financial beliefs and goals are compatible.

TRUE OR FALSE 10. My guy and I openly share information about ourselves with each other.

TRUE OR FALSE 11. On occasion I have witnessed my guy treating other people disrespectfully.

TRUE OR FALSE 12. We have a lot of stress in our relationship and often don't have good strategies for dealing with it.

TRUE OR FALSE 13. When we discuss important issues, I feel like he always thinks he knows more than me.

TRUE OR FALSE 14. When we fight it always seems like he needs to win the argument.

TRUE OR FALSE 15. I am a better person (stronger, healthier, more ambitious, happier, etc.) when I am with him than when we are apart.

TRUE OR FALSE 16. His best friend is someone other than me.

TRUE OR FALSE 17. He is focused more on our friendship than on sex.

TRUE OR FALSE 18. We avoid talking about serious matters.

TRUE OR FALSE 19. He sometimes bullies his friends, family, pets, and/or me.

TRUE OR FALSE 20. He is the first person I would go to with good news, bad news, a problem that I can't solve, etc.

TRUE OR FALSE 21. I have occasional doubts about the depth of my love for him.

TRUE OR FALSE   22. I feel like I know everything about him that I need to know.

TRUE OR FALSE   23. He regularly says hurtful things to me that I wish he wouldn't say.

TRUE OR FALSE   24. Sometimes I wonder if he can be totally committed to our relationship for the rest of our lives.

TRUE OR FALSE   25. I have found that sometimes his actions do not match his words.

TRUE OR FALSE   26. He nearly always follows through with the important things he says he is going to do.

TRUE OR FALSE   27. He listens to me and respects my opinions.

TRUE OR FALSE   28. The two of us frequently use words like I, me and mine rather than we, us and our.

TRUE OR FALSE   29. Our relationship always comes before his family or friends.

TRUE OR FALSE   30. He is happiest in our relationship when he makes the final decisions.

TRUE OR FALSE   31. When we argue, name-calling and insults are frequently used.

TRUE OR FALSE   32. Both of us have similar attitudes about matters of spirituality.

TRUE OR FALSE   33. I trust him completely with everything, including my life, my money, my reputation and my dreams.

The answers to this quiz can be found in APPENDIX A on page 229.

THE FORWARD

Having often been asked the question, "What is the best predictor of a great marriage?" the Doctors' answer is always the same, "Marry the right guy in the first place." While this may sound glib, during interviews with the Doctors women report *knowing* that they married the right guy or unfortunately the wrong guy soon after the wedding. Why didn't these women recognize the telltale issues before they said, "I Do?"

Every woman wants to marry the right guy, but very few women know what to look for, how to ask the right questions, how to engage her potential spouse in discussions about essential issues and what actually matters. Women want to know which tough questions they should ask, the answers to listen for, what really matters in a relationship, and the essential issues to discuss with their potential spouse before saying, "I do."

How to Marry the Right Guy poses 33 critical questions and guides a woman through getting ready to accept love, assessing whether she has actually found the right guy, determining what really matters in her relationship and deciding when she is truly ready to get married. With this research-based knowledge, women can greatly enhance their chances of selecting the right man and living happily ever after.

How to Marry the Right Guy is the "have-to-have" book for every woman who thinks she has found the right guy and is contemplating marriage. Women will relate well to the positive message, critical questions, short quality answers, essential discussion issues, and practical relationship tips offered in this book from a credible team in the relationship and marriage education field, who have been married themselves for 47 years.

One final note, while this book is organized around several important themes, it does not necessarily have to be read in sequential order. It is perfectly acceptable to "skip around" to topics of burning interest to you.

INTRODUCTION

HOW TO MARRY THE RIGHT GUY

Introduction
Marry the Right Guy in the First Place

*D*ID YOU EVER WONDER WHY some women find the perfect guy to marry, do so, and enjoy a love affair that lasts a lifetime? On the other hand, some women marry a guy that is wrong for them now, wrong for them tomorrow, and wrong for them for a lifetime? What's the difference? Why do some women succeed at love and marriage when others fail?

One of our mentors, Don Clifton, the former CEO of the world renowned Gallup Organization (rest his soul), often reminded us of the power of "pervasive personality characteristics." Don defined "pervasive" as "a recurring pattern of thought and behavior." In other words, these are the personality characteristics that a human being develops within the first two decades of life that, for the most part, defines who they are for a lifetime. Don believed that you are what you are by the time you become an adult. Changing who and what you are becomes nearly impossible after that.

So what is the lesson in all this? Simple really. The people you meet in life are, by the time they reach adulthood, pretty much what they are. They won't change much, if at all. The hard truth is, they can't change who they really are, even if they wanted to. Oh, sure, people as adults can make you believe from time to time that they are something different than what they really are, but in the end, they are what they are. Make no mistake about that.

When it comes to love and marriage, there is a truism that trumps all truisms. It goes like this—pay close and careful attention to the words, deeds, and actions of the guy you think you are falling in love with. And in the end, pay most of your attention to his actions, first and foremost! The truth is, a guy's actions speak so much louder than his words. Never lose sight of this truism for to do so is to put your heart, your health, and your happiness at peril.

One of the questions we are most often asked as we travel the world discussing our work and conducting our marriage interviews is this: "What are the secrets of a successful marriage?" Our immediate answer is always the same—marry the right person!

On the surface this may seem like a flippant answer to such a serious question, but it isn't really. If a woman who thinks she is falling in love with a guy would pay more attention to his actions and not the words, she wouldn't miss the telltale signs.

Here's how it works. You think you love a guy. He tells you all of the right things. But over time you begin to notice that his actions belie his words. He tells you he respects you but dismisses your opinions. He waxes on about how he puts you on a pedestal but never opens the door for you when he gets to it first. He tells you how he wants the relationship between the two of you a shared relationship, and then he makes all the decisions. You get the idea. We could go on.

The point is this—if you fail to notice and question the actions of the one you purport to love in the early stages of your relationship then you are deluding yourself into thinking he will change later on. Guys rarely do. And so often, women who ignore the warning signs end up getting married, only to discover later on that the guy they married is not who they thought he was.

So, back to the earlier question—the best secret to a successful marriage is marrying the right guy in the first place! Taking the time to carefully observe the actions of the guy you think you love over a period of time tells you a lot more about him than his words ever could. All too often we hear a woman lament to us that if she had only paid attention to the telltale signs, she would not have married the person she married. Many of these relationships end in divorce.

Paying close and careful attention to the guy you are thinking about marrying in the early stages of your relationship can save a failed marriage from happening in the first place. This is the ultimate key to a successful marriage.

We don't mean to suggest that it is always easy to tell if the one you think you love is one you can have a successful marriage with. We do, however, believe strongly that using the Marry the Right Guy Quiz and learning the 33 indicators can help you know what to look for.

If you consciously and rationally believe that the words, deeds, and actions of the guy you are thinking of marrying are consistent and he passes all of 33 indicators predicting a successful marriage, then your marriage has a great chance for success.

Making a marriage a success requires hard work. If you base your marriage on a lie—you ignored the actions you were observing in the guy you were falling in love with—then all of the simple things required to make a marriage work will more than likely not be enough for you to live happily ever after in marital bliss.

Pervasive characteristics in people are very real. They define who they are and they almost never change. As we always say, keep your eyes wide open when you are falling in love. You won't regret it later.

One final note—never enter a marriage thinking you can ignore his behaviors now and change them later. Too many women have fallen prey to this notion. It rarely ever works.

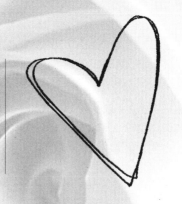

THE RIGHT YOU

HOW TO MARRY THE RIGHT GUY

C H A P T E R 1

Why should the "Right You" come first?

Every little girl wants to marry
Prince Charming, but the truth is
finding the "Right You"
has to come first.

HEN IT COMES TO finding the right guy to marry, "The Right You" comes first. You can't respect someone else unless you show respect for yourself.

Every little girl wants to marry Prince Charming and live happily ever after. But no one tells you how. It is a discovery process that sometimes goes very wrong because the focus was on Prince Charming before the girl is prepared for true love.

Becoming the right you has to come first. You have to love yourself before you can love someone else. Discovering your strengths, being the best you can be and liking yourself, form the foundation for a lasting relationship.

Here are seven major steps that need to be completed before you are ready to find the guy of your dreams that you can spend the rest of your life with:

1. **Get healthy—mentally and physically.** Take time to heal and stabilize from any bad relationships. You can't make appropriate decisions "off-balance" or in an unhealthy state. Get healthy first! You will be much better served. The best decisions in life come when you are healthy. Believe us when we say this!

2. **Focus on the positive and extinguish negative thoughts and behaviors.** Count your blessings and enjoy what you have. If you have friends and family who love you unconditionally, you already have more than most people have in this world. Take stock of the things in your life that really matter and then focus on what you have rather than what you want. Stop whatever behaviors are dragging you down. That means if you are a heavy drinker, a smoker, a gambler, a shopaholic, or an overeater, stop. If you constantly worry about what will happen tomorrow or you dwell on the things people do wrong, or . . . Whatever you do that gets you into a bad mood or adversely affects your well being, make a concerted effort to extinguish those behaviors and thoughts.

3. **Develop your interests and hobbies.** What makes you happy? What activity gives you pleasure? It is exercising, or reading, or canoeing, or traveling? Make time in your schedule to engage in those activities. Master your special interest or hobby until you feel quite

proud of what you can do or what you know about it. You become a much more interesting and attractive person when you have your own interests, hobbies and skills.

4. **Get your financial house in order.** If you have run up debt and your month is longer than your paycheck can handle, reduce your spending habits and make a plan to pay down your debt as rapidly as possible. Get professional financial help if you need it. But don't look for a Prince Charming to gallop up and perform a daring rescue. Celebrate each success such as paying off a credit card.

5. **Be ready to give love unconditionally.** Knowing that love is a gift, you need to be able to feel good about giving love away with no expectation of getting anything in return. To do this takes real confidence and trust in yourself.

6. **Look for love in the right places.** Recognize that your real love will come along when you find someone who shares your interests. You need to develop your interests—be it kayaking, camping out, social events at your place of worship, dancing, or whatever strikes your fancy. You need to find your comfort zone—a place where you can find happiness. You are much more likely to attract a potential mate if you go to places where the likelihood exists that there are others there who share your interests.

7. **The best things in life come your way when you least expect them**—when you are content to let nature take its course. The "butterfly of life" has this simple

lesson—if you find yourself in a meadow and there are butterflies all around, always remember, if you grab at the butterfly, it will fly away. If you just sit under a tall Oak Tree and enjoy all the love the butterfly brings, it will gently land on your shoulder. Don't try so hard to find love. Be patient and it will come your way.

We hope that you find your new love and that you find him soon. Having companionship is one of the most cherished gifts of life and love. Never forget these simple lessons for finding true love.

CHAPTER 2

What matters most to you?

*When you know what
matters most to you, you are
ready to determine what
you want in a life partner.*

*B*EFORE YOU CAN DETERMINE
if a guy is the right guy to marry, you have to know what matters
most to you. What do you care deeply about? What are your core
values?

When you know what matters most to you, you are ready to
determine what you want in a life partner. Assuring that his core
values match yours is critical in the process of deciding if the two of
you will have a love that can last for a lifetime.

No love has blossomed or been sustained without the two individuals in the relationship agreeing on their core values, what they
care deeply about, and what they are committed to doing together.

What are the core values that matter in great relationships?

In spite of enormous challenges from time to time, the best marriages survive and thrive. They survive and thrive because they are committed to a set of core values present in all great marriages and successful loving relationships. See if your core values match those given by couples with happy marriages throughout the world:

1. **The couple in love is committed to always putting each other first in their relationship with each other.** The first thing you notice in all highly successful loving relationships is that those who purport to be in love recognize that their relationship is not about you and me, it is about US. Discovering that YOU are not the center of the universe is the hallmark of a great relationship. Actually putting another human being number one is a powerful indication that you are truly in love.

2. **The couple in love is committed to democracy in their relationship.** Always remember, successful loving relationships are egalitarian. Namely, the best relationships understand that theirs is a shared relationship. If one person has all the power and makes all the decisions, it is NOT love! True love is a very democratic thing!

3. **The couple in love is committed to ensuring their mutual happiness.** Remember, true love is not just about ensuring your happiness. More importantly, and often for the first time in your life, you actually enjoy and are motivated by ensuring the happiness of someone other than yourself. It is a good feeling!

4. **The couple in love values absolute trustworthiness and integrity in their relationship with each other.** If you cannot trust the one you love, then it is not true love! The most successful loving relationships report that they trust their mate unequivocally and without hesitation. To violate that trust is to undermine and, ultimately destroy, the relationship with the one you say you love.

5. **The couple in love is committed to caring and unconditional love for each other.** When you truly love someone you do so without conditions. It is not about loving you IF . . . True love is unconditional.

6. **The couple in love is committed to being mutually respectful towards each other.** There is a Golden Rule in true love and it is like the one you learned early in your life, "Do unto others as you would have them do unto you." Do not expect to be treated with respect when you are disrespectful to the one you love. Respectfulness is at the heart of all great loving relationships.

7. **The couple in love values their mutual sense of responsibility for each other.** A person in love cares for the one they love in ways that they have never cared for another human being. They feel a sense of responsibility for another person that they have never felt before. It feels so good to put another's needs above your own. To do so is to love deeply.

The core values of all successful loving relationships are at the heart of the matter. If you and your mate are committed to these values, your love has a good chance of thriving over your lifetime together.

After thinking about the core values revealed to us by the thousands of happily married couples we have interviewed around the world, you need to take the next step to carefully ascertain what matters most to you.

What do you care deeply about?

Knowing what you really care deeply about is an essential step to discovering whether the man you think you are in love with is the right guy for you. If you care deeply about the environment and the guy you think you are in love with is not committed to recycling or taking care of nature, he will have great difficulty respecting what you believe in. If you are a person who cares deeply for animals and he feels uncomfortable being around animals, your relationship will have difficulty blossoming into a lifetime of love together.

Here are some starter questions to ask yourself:

1. **What matters most to me? Number your top 5 in priority order:**

- Family

- Religion and faith

- Nature

- Animals

- Education

- Peace and quiet

- Adventure

- Romance

- Music

- Theater

- Money

- Helping people

- Travel

- Food

- Health

- Fashion

- Home

- World News and Events

- Others—list other choices if in your top 5

2. **What activities do you enjoy doing so much that you would not feel satisfied if you were not able to do them? Number your top 5 in priority order:**

- Exercising

- Playing sports

- Watching sports

- Reading

- Socializing or going to parties

- Cooking

- Doing arts or crafts

- Traveling

- Dining out

- Having conversations

- Watching movies or television

- Collecting stamps, coins, miniatures, etc.

- Gardening

- Shopping

- Building things
- Charity work
- Others—list other choices if in your top 5

3. **What matters most to you in the guy you would like to marry? Number your top 5 in priority order:**

- Honesty
- Business Sense
- Good Athlete
- Great Social Skills
- Integrity
- Caring Personality
- Dependable
- Hard Worker
- Politically Astute
- Artistic
- Lover of the Arts
- World Traveler
- Similar Interests and Hobbies
- Great Looking
- Good Family Man
- Others—list other choices if in your top 5

While these are only a beginning, they will get you started in your quest for what matters most to you. By truly knowing yourself, what you believe in, and what matters most to you, you will be ready to determine if the guy you think you love has compatible beliefs and core values.

CHAPTER 3

Can you let go of past relationships?

It is downright challenging to get over past relationships.

*W*E KNOW HOW YOU FEEL. Starting over is really difficult when it comes to love. Experiencing a bad relationship, breaking up, or losing the one you love can be overwhelmingly painful.

The simple truth is this—you entered into a relationship with another person expecting it to last. But all acts of love are, we are afraid to say, not everlasting.

As the old song goes, "Breaking up is hard to do." Whether that breakup is due to you falling out of love or the one you love moving on, the pain is still not minimized. It is hard to start over. It is downright challenging to get over past relationships.

If you are faced with developing a new loving relationship, there are some simple truths that will help you make the appropriate transition to a new love. Here are the five tips to help you let go of past relationships:

1. **Understand, you cannot find love on the rebound.** Don't get in a hurry to find your next love. Doing so will only lead to disaster and disillusionment. Be patient. If you think you have already found the next love of your life when you are still on the rebound, be especially careful and take the time to match his actions and words with the 33 questions in the How to Marry the Right Guy Quiz.

2. **Analyze what you could do differently in your next relationship.** Ending a relationship almost always has both individuals blaming each other. However, if you are truthful with yourself, there are things you could have done differently that would have made the relationship better. If you spend time thinking about your actions and reactions in the context of your failed relationship, you can begin processing what you could do differently in your next relationship that will add to the chances that it will last for a lifetime.

3. **Keep the thoughts of your past relationships off your mind.** Now that you have analyzed what you could do differently, stop thinking about your past relationships. We know, that isn't as easy as it sounds. But, it is important to take that step and let go of your negative, longing, or wistful thoughts about your past relationships. Whenever you begin thinking about one of your past relationships, take a deep breath and begin thinking about your favorite song, place, book,

or movie. Think about anything that will get our mind off your past relationship.

4. **Be content—enjoy what you have!** If you have good health, a great pet, financial stability, a good job, or friends and family who love you unconditionally, you already have more than most people have in this world. Appreciate what you have rather than long for something else. The simple act of being content with your life and what you have gives you a sense of satisfaction that radiates for others to see. Take stock of the things in your life that really matter and then focus on your blessings.

5. **Find out what makes you happy.** No one is more enjoyable to be around than someone who is happy. What makes you happy? What makes you enjoy life? What gives you pleasure and satisfaction? When you can answer those questions and invest more time doing the things that make you happy and less time doing those things that make you unhappy, you will attract others to you.

New horizons will open up as you begin to let go of the past negative relationships and focus on your new opportunities or your new love. Having companionship is one of the most cherished gifts of life and love. Letting go of past relationships will allow you to be ready to embrace a new love that can truly provide you with a lifetime of happiness with the right guy.

୭୧

CHAPTER 4

Are you healthy enough to engage in love?

An important predictor of mental health is nutritional intake or lack thereof!

*M*AKE NO MISTAKE ABOUT it—what we eat, drink, and otherwise ingest into our bodies has a significant effect on both our physical and mental health.

The couples we have interviewed around the world who have great marriages talk about the importance of being healthy in BOTH a physical AND mental sense. Don't shortchange yourself and your chances of sustaining a lasting love by thinking your health doesn't matter.

If someone told you that the lack of Vitamin C could lead to Scurvy, you would say, "Everybody knows that!"

If someone told you that the lack of proper levels of Folic Acid in pregnant women could lead to Autism in the child that is born, you would agree. The evidence in support of this notion seems pretty overwhelming.

Unless you have been living under a rock for the past 50 years, you know that proper nutrition is essential for good PHYSICAL health. No one disputes this simple notion.

Yet, when you extend the notion of proper nutrition to mental health, some folks look at you like a deer in the headlights of your car! They ask, "Huh?" What could nutrition possibly have to do with good mental health and a great relationship? Why do so many believe that proper nutrition only applies to good physical health and not to good mental health?

According to the *Diagnostic and Statistical Manual of Mental Disorders (DSM-IV-TR, Fourth Edition)*, "...4 out of the 10 leading causes of disability in the US and other developed countries are mental disorders. Major depression, bipolar disorder, schizophrenia, and obsessive-compulsive disorder (OCD) are among the most common mental disorders that currently plague numerous countries and have varying incidence rates." Many scientists believe that the root causes of several of these diseases are nutritionally based.

Studies show that a lack of certain dietary nutrients contributes to the development of mental and associated disorders. For example, essential vitamins such as vitamin C and the B vitamins, certain minerals, and the omega-3 fatty acids, have been found to be deficient in patients suffering from mental disorders, including depression. Unfortunately, these vitamins are often deficient in the general population in America and other developed countries.

A number of years ago, Charley taught a special seminar course entitled, "Nutrition and Mental Health." He admitted a half-dozen, carefully selected graduate students, and they began a journey to discover the truth about the relationship between mental health and proper nutrition.

They collected data for a good part of a semester from a myriad of international sources. The class then compared their findings about mental health and nutrition to selected scales of the well-known and much used Minnesota Multiphasic Personality Inventory (MMPI).

To the astonishment of Charley and his students, the correlation between nutrition and mental health was overwhelming. They took their results and created what they called the "Psycho-Nutrition Inventory" (PNI, 1983).

The simple truth they discovered was this—the single best predictor of selected scale scores on the MMPI was the PNI. Translation—the best predictor of mental health was nutritional intake, or lack thereof!

Imagine the surprise and joy over this important discovery! The best predictor of mental health was a score on an inventory that measured nutritional levels! Does the word "breakthrough" come to mind?

To quote from Charley's study in 1983 (which still holds true today):

> "Namely, there is a sufficient amount of evidence available in the Orthomolecular research literature to suggest that a maladjusted person is certainly not going to get better psychologically if he/she continues to exhibit nutritionally maladaptive behaviors. Clearly, if maladjusted clients can learn to effectively

control those nutritional and corollary habits that increase their mental unhealthiness, as defined by psycho/ nutrition theory, then they at least have a fighting chance to become healthy through the utilization of other treatment strategies employed by the counselor."

The human body is a very complex entity. But the truth is, those who separate mind and body in their analysis of the human being are just plain wrong—just plain out of touch with the realities of what it means to be human!

Here's the deal—in order to sustain a quality relationship with the one you love you need to have good mental health. In order to maintain good mental health you need to engage in proper nutrition – you need to eat healthy and engage in healthy activities! Virtually all of the "rules" you hear about healthy eating and healthy living for a healthy "physical body" also apply to a healthy "mental body." The elixir of good health is exercise, healthy eating, and nutritional supplementation to fill in the holes.

Recognizing that your health is critical to your relationship, both short-term and long-term, allows you to focus on the five areas essential to developing healthy living habits. If you are young, there is a tendency to ignore the health risk factors because you think you will live forever. Instead, begin thinking long-term and focus on developing healthy habits both physically and mentally.

The seven keys to developing healthy living habits:

1. **Fix healthy meals.** Find recipes that are fun to fix and fun to eat. A good way to start is to try a few of the salad recipes we have included in Appendix F of this book. These are recipes from happily married couples all over the world who realized that healthy eating benefitted their relationship with each other.

2. **Develop a regular exercise program together.** It doesn't matter if it is just walking in the evening after work or riding bicycles in the park or going to the gym or swimming. What matters is that you commit to staying on a regular program to enhance your physical and mental health. Yes, exercise does have a positive impact on your mental health.

3. **Focus on maintaining good psychological health.** Life can throw unbelievable challenges in your path. The mental strength you develop in yourself and your positive attitude about life will make you a better partner for the one you love. If the guy you are thinking about marrying is the right guy, he is also your best friend. The psychological support you can provide each other will take you through the tough times. Like the song goes, "that's what friends are for."

4. **For a long and healthy life, take a balanced regimen of vitamins.** Don't fool yourself into believing that you will get all of your nutrition by eating a well balanced diet. While it might help, with the stress in today's life it is critical that you make sure that you get the required vitamins and minerals with a good vitamin supplement.

5. **Eliminate bad habits.** In other words, cut back on your foods containing refined sugars, white flour, salt, food additives such as food coloring, artificial flavorings and preservatives. Stop smoking. Limit your intact of alcohol to 1-2 drinks per day. Get off the couch. Get more consistent sleep.

6. **Get regular annual medical check-ups.** Get a regular physical check-up annually. Preventative care is far

superior to dealing with a health issue that went undetected for a long period of time.

7. **Make living a healthy well-balanced life a priority.** Just like everything else in life, you have to set your goals and priorities focused on what is important to you. While you may not have any health issues yet, if you develop healthy living habits that focus on maintaining a healthy well-balanced life style, you have a far greater chance of enjoying a long and healthy life.

Over these past 31 years, we have studied successful marriages on all 7 of the world's continents, in 48 countries, and in all 50 of these United States. Make no mistake about it—good mental and physical health is of paramount importance for a "healthy" and successful relationship.

The way you emote, your anxiety, your productivity, and your ability to engage in a loving relationship, are all affected by what you put into your mouth (or do not!) and how you maintain the health of your body—both mentally and physically. The importance you place on how you manage your mind and mood through food, exercise, and healthy living will make a difference in maintaining the relationship with the right guy you choose to marry.

Don't worry. Be healthy. Be happy.

CHAPTER 5

How will you know you are really in love?

*It is like watching a pair of ice dancers
gliding through a perfectly executed lift—
they are beautiful skaters individually,
but magnificent when together.*

*I*N OUR MANY INTERVIEWS WITH
couples "in love" we ask them, perhaps, the most revealing question
of the interview, "How did you know you were really in love?" We
have heard very consistent answers. And conversely, many people
involved in a new loving relationship, particularly young people,
often ask us, "How will I know if I am really in love?"

While we have heard a number of answers to our "How did you
know you were in love" question, we can place the answers into
seven categories. And, perhaps surprisingly, they have stayed the
same over our more than 30 years of research with couples in love.

In a nutshell, here are the first signs that you are really in love:

1. **Physical:** People who say they are in love report getting "goose bumps," "a palpating heart," "sweaty palms," "a lump in my throat," "teary-eyed when I say goodbye," "a tingling sensation all over my body." People in love have a positive physical reaction when they think about or see the one they love.

2. **Emotional:** When they think about or see the person they love most lovers report "an uncontrollable smile comes over my face whenever I see him," and "I laugh more often when I am with the person I love," and "I miss him when he leaves the room." People in love feel emotions for the person they love that they do not routinely feel for others.

3. **Positive worry:** Over the years, we continue to be amazed about the consistency with which people in love report to us that they "worry about their lover" when they are not around. Little thoughts of what we have come to call "positive worry" about the one they love begins to creep into their mind—things like car accidents, falling down, getting hurt at work, and getting sick. The folks we interview for the most part do not worry compulsively or negatively. These thoughts are normal and natural when you are "in love."

4. **I-cannot-imagine-life-without-him:** This is the point in love when you begin to think about the future—your future with the one you love. When you cannot imagine your life without him, you are in love!

5. **Oneness of your relationship:** You begin to realize that you truly want him in your life. Everything changes from thoughts of you, me, I, and my to WE! You truly feel like the person you love makes you want to be the best you can be. They lift you to higher goals and make you feel complete because they are your best supporter and cheerleader. When the feeling of oneness consumes your body you are in love!

6. **Pre-occupied love:** Simply stated, you think about him most of the time. You want to be with him. You want to share with him. You want to live with him, share a bed with him, hold him and hug him. You actually begin to think more about him than about yourself or your needs. You think about his wants, his needs, his desires and his love.

7. **Love itself and your ability to express that love:** You finally have the courage to tell him you love him! You miss him when he is not around. You worry about him. You care about his safety and welfare. You suddenly and out of nowhere are inspired to say I LOVE YOU! I LOVE YOU! I LOVE YOU! You shout it to the stars. You are in love!

While these seven first signs reveal if you are really in love, they do not determine if the man you are in love with is the man you can live with happily ever after. You will need to address each of the 33 critical questions before you can make the determination as to whether the guy you are in love with is the right guy for you to marry.

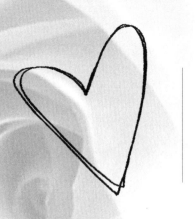

THE RIGHT GUY

HOW TO MARRY THE RIGHT GUY

Can you change him?

There are seven fatal personality
characteristics to watch for
in the man you are
thinking about marrying.

OUR FAVORITE QUESTIONS
for a woman whose marriage has failed are: WHY? What went
wrong? Why do you think your marriage failed?

The answer we often get from our female respondents is this, "I
thought I could fix him." We wish she had asked us about this issue
before she decided she could change him into "Mr. Right."

There is one truism you can take to the bank, YOU CANNOT
CHANGE HIM! Either accept him the way he is—warts and all—
or move on.

Always remember, the personality of a human being is WELL established by their early to late teen years! If you think you can change him, you are potentially setting yourself up for an unsatisfying and failed relationship . . . and often times, with dangerous consequences.

There are many red flags in a relationship that you need to look for. There are character flaws you must be aware of.

In our thousands of interviews we have learned that there are seven telltale signs of relationships that will not work. These are not habits such as burping after dinner, leaving messes around the house, or turning the music up too loud. These are pervasive personality characteristics you cannot CHANGE or FIX. Don't be fooled and don't be deluded into thinking you can make these attitudes and behaviors go away. You can't!

Memorize these characteristics. Doing so could save you from a life of unhappiness, distress, and, very often, danger. If the one you purport to love demonstrates any of these in your daily interactions with him, strongly consider moving on with your life—truly consider finding another man to spend your life with.

Here are the seven fatal personality characteristics to watch for:

1. **Controlling Behavior:** We often hear women say to us "He always wants to be in charge." He wants to "Have the last word." "If I say left, he says right!" "If I want to go to movie X, he buys tickets for movie Y." He wants to control who you talk to, what you do and where you go. The simple truth of the matter is this – he wants to be in charge. Behaviors tell us a story, of that you can be sure. When your guy exhibits behaviors that telegraph to you he wants to be in charge of your relationship, be very wary! He has no right to be

in charge. A true loving relationship does not have bosses. True loving relationships are characterized by adherence to democracy—a relationship where responsibility is shared. Having someone "in charge" does not make for a healthy relationship. Learn this lesson well!

2. **Condescending Attitude:** Here's the deal—your guy is NOT your master, ladies! You are not his slave. And frankly, there is no hierarchy in a loving relationship. He is not more important than you. His attitudes and opinions do not trump yours. It would be silly to suppress your feelings and opinions because you think he is smarter than you. If he exhibits a condescending attitude towards you more than once a week, you might want to reconsider your relationship with him. There are no feelings of superiority in successful loving relationships. Love and friendship are all about equality. If he acts like he is superior, it is time for you to move on!

3. **Narcissistic Behavior:** According to the Mayo Clinic, "Narcissistic personality disorder is a mental disorder in which people have an inflated sense of their own importance and a deep need for admiration." Those with narcissistic personality disorder believe that they're superior to others and have little regard for other people's feelings. This is a serious red flag to be cautious about. Men with narcissistic personalities cannot be changed!

Many women we have interviewed tell us that their so-called "partner" believes everything should be about him and that he has an insatiable need for admiration and self-aggrandizement. In his mind, he is more important than her. But here is the simple truth—no human being is superior to another! If he thinks he is superior to you, you should demonstrate otherwise by walking away from your relationship with him. It really is that simple.

4. **Bullying Tactics:** Let's be honest here—nobody likes a bully. We have all seen them. Many of us have dealt with them over the years. There are bullies on the school playground. There are bullies at work. And sadly, there is a bully in many marriages and in many relationships. There are bullies everywhere, make no mistake about it. A bully wants to push you around. A bully wants to show you that they are in charge of YOU! A bully wants to make you cower in his presence. A bully is a termite. He is always trying to get inside of you and weaken you. He wants to eat away at your interior so he can control you. So, we ask this simple question, "Does your mate bully you?" If he does, it is time to walk away from your relationship.

5. **Manipulative Actions:** Here is a simple question for you to contemplate—does the one you love try to manipulate you? Does he try to "pull your strings" as if you were a puppet? Does he try to exercise power over you through his manipulation of the situation? And more importantly, does he continuously find different ways to manipulate you—your actions, your feelings, your behaviors, and your aspirations? The divorced women we have interviewed over the years tell us that their failed relationship was, more than anything, the result of her ex's manipulation of

them—his lack of appreciation for her free will, her ability to make her own decisions. Some men always want to steer you towards a conclusion they would have drawn, not one you would have drawn. Beware of manipulation!

6. **Lack of Follow Through:** Okay, he promised you a rose garden, but never delivered! He told you he would take you to dinner, but made excuses for why he didn't do it. He told you he would cut the grass, but didn't. He told you he would be there by 8:00, but didn't show up until 10:00. He told you he would do the shopping, but didn't. The truth is, he told you he would do a lot of things. In the end, he rarely ever follows through on his promises. Let's face it many men have no follow-through. You cannot depend on them to do what they say they will do. Heed the warnings—not following through is a warning sign that you should pay close and careful attention to.

7. **Cannot be Trusted:** We have found over the years that the best marriages have at their core—TRUST! If you can't trust the one you love, you are in deep doo-doo. Trust us on this (pardon the pun). During our thousands of interviews around the world, we are continuously reminded of the centrality of trust to the most successful marital relationships. In those marriages that survive over time, they all report to us that their undying trust for each other carried them through the good times and the bad. Trust is at the heart of every happily married couple's relationship.

If you have caught the man you think you are love in lies—even little lies—be very cautious. Brushing it off as no big deal can have major consequences. If he talks about how he doesn't have to be truthful with his friends or family members in certain circumstances, be very cautious. If he can lie to a friend or family member, he will lie to you.

And always remember this—infidelity destroys more marriages and loving relationships than any other single act. Infidelity is based upon being able to lie effectively. If you can't trust him, move on. If you stay, you do so at your peril.

Here is the most important lesson of all—if he is flawed, if his actions and behaviors correspond to any of the aforementioned seven fatal flaws, you have to understand that you cannot fix him! If he demonstrates any of these pervasive personality characteristics, he is impossible to change. If you want to flail away at windmills, go ahead and believe that you can change him. But in the end, you will be terribly disappointed.

Personality is formed early in life. People rarely change. Their actions do, in fact, trump their words. Remember that truism that mothers have been saying to their children forever, *"Actions speak louder than words."*

CHAPTER   7

Can you trust him?

*You can tell a lot about
a man by his actions.
Words are cheap.
Actions mean everything!*

*I*N OUR THOUSANDS OF
interviews with happily married couples, we are always struck by
their undying trust in each other. They literally trust each other
with their lives, their entire wellbeing, and their sacred honor.

The words they use to describe the one they love more often
than not include words and expressions like trust, honesty, loyalty,
respects me, admires me, always there for me, never lets me down,
truthful, and never lies to me. Their trust for each other is about as
complete as you can get. And when we ask couples in love during
our interviews to place, in an overall sense, where their relationship

is on a 10-point scale with 10 being "Absolute Trust," without exception, they say "10!" Isn't that remarkably wonderful?

Unfortunately, all too often in life people fall in love blindly. They refuse to make note of how the actions of another person define them. They pay too much attention to words and way too little to actions.

Here is an undeniable truth about people—actions speak louder than words! We know, you've heard this all before! But the truth is, you can, and must, judge a man by his actions and NOT by his words!

Words are cheap. Actions mean everything! The truth is always there for all to see when you observe the way people act and respond, rarely by what they say. Good men practice what they preach. Here's why.

In answer to the question, "Can you trust him?" you must always remember this—you can tell a lot about a man by his actions. How does he respond to you? How does he treat you? How does he treat your friends, your family, his dog, and all of the other people and things you love? How does he treat the janitor, the person who cuts your grass, or the checker at the supermarket?

Real men say what they mean and act the same way. Real men, good men, decent men, will always demonstrate who they are by their consistent actions. To know the real truth about a man—pay close and careful attention to him over a period of several weeks and then ask yourself this question—is he really what he appears to be? Consistent actions on his part will tell you what you need to know, for good or for bad.

Lately, we have been working with a couple who have been married for nearly 22 years and they are calling it quits. Why just today, she told us that it was time to get out of the relationship—

time to "fish or cut bait." For nearly 22 years, her husband had mentally abused her and the children, while all the time boasting about how much he loved them. Actions speak louder than words!

The truth is, you can't really love your children when you constantly berate them. You can't truly love anyone that you put down, yell at, or constantly point out their failings and their frailties.

When you love someone, you learn to live with their failings, their mistakes, and their transgressions. In the end, you love them for what they are—for what they are in their heart and in their soul.

We all make mistakes. We all do dumb things from time to time. And the truth is, we more often than not, recover from the shortcomings we have. Honest, one-time mistakes are forgivable. On the other hand, repeated actions reveal who a person really is—for good or for bad.

A psychologist friend of ours reminds us from time to time about the "pervasive characteristics" present in human beings. These are "recurring patterns of thought and behavior" that defines a person – that tells us who they are. And recurring patterns of thought and behavior for the most part do not change when a person is an adult. In reality, these pervasive characteristics define who you are. Oh, sure, some people can cover up their real personality characteristics from time to time, but if you observe them long enough you will learn who they really are.

When someone you are observing over time repeatedly and consistently demonstrates through their actions and deeds the pervasive characteristics present in them you must pay attention! If a man is truly a good person you can trust, then you will see it in their actions. Don't be fooled by words that are contrary to their actions.

When you fall in love make it for all the right reasons. Don't ignore the signs. Don't ignore the glitches. Pay attention and your reward will, more often than not, be true love with a man you can trust. Ignore his actions and you do so at your own peril.

Trust is not something all loving relationships start with. For some couples the trust becomes complete in a few years. For others, it takes awhile. But one thing is for sure; happy and successful marriages and relationships survive and thrive on the basis of this trust. Trust is so pervasive in their relationship that they never give it a second thought. They expect it. It's always there. It is part of the fabric of their relationship.

You see, character in a successful marriage or relationship does matter, and character is about trust. Being honest and trustworthy is at the heart of all the best loving relationships we have studied. It really is a 10 on a 10-point scale. In our estimation, character is the foundation of true love! Therefore, character in the man you love is an essential ingredient for lasting love.

CHAPTER 8

Is he your best friend?

*No relationship has ever
passed the test of time.
without friendship.*

*W*E HAVE HEARD IT SO
many times in our interviews with those who say they are in love, "I
love my partner." "I love my fiancée." "I love my spouse." I love, I
love! But is love enough? Can love really sustain your relationship?
This is the most important question you can ask yourself.

We have heard this popular refrain over and over. We admit it—
people who say they are in love, probably are! But is love enough
to sustain the best relationships?

Here's the rub—being IN love is easy. It expresses an emotion
common to those relationships that have transcended time. Being
in love is central to the best marriages—to the best relationships
between two people. But being in love is NOT enough!

Here is what we know from our thousands of interviews with those who have had a successful and long-lasting relationship with another human being—no relationship has ever passed the test of time without **friendship.**

One of the questions of our interview protocol is this, "Who is your best friend?" While we ask this question in every interview, there are two answers that stand out for us as to the importance of friendship in the best relationships.

We got our first most telling response in Rio de Janiero. After asking this question of the so-called "Best Couple in Rio" we got answers that drove home this point to us. When we asked the most prominent physician in the magnificent city of Rio who his best friend was, he named TEN people and NONE was his wife of 37 years!

And it gets worse—when we asked his wife who her best friend was, she gave ten names and, like him, the list of names did not include her husband, the prominent physician she had been married to for the same 37 years!

Here's another good example of our point. When we interviewed a couple in Sydney, Australia a few years ago, as usual, we asked the same question, "Who is your best friend?"

To our surprise, both people in this so-called loving relationship, did not consider each other their best friend. We probed and we probed, but alas, neither would admit that their spouse was their best friend.

The simple truth of the matter is this—these two couples professed to "love" each other, but they did not "like" each other. They were clearly not best friends. In fact, when we asked clarifying questions, it became quite clear that neither couple had friendship within their respective relationships.

Make no mistake about it—loving someone is NOT enough. If they are not your best friend, your relationship with them will not pass the test of time. Your relationship with them can never be judged as a great success.

You see, the standard principle in the most successful relationships around the world is this—your partner IS your best friend! There is no equivocation when it comes to this point. Best friends provide each other total trust, loyalty, mutual respect, admiration, encouragement, support, caring, and much more.

If the one you love is not your best friend, your relationship is in serious trouble and, in all likelihood, will not become one of the lifelong love stories we have heard around the world on all seven continents.

So, we will ask you what we have asked every couple we have interviewed across the continents—is the one you purport to love really your best friend? If they are not, you are not really in love for a lifetime.

In the best marriages and loving relationships, being best friends trumps everything else. There are no if's, and's, or but's about it.

Love well! More importantly, like well!

Are your core values
and virtues compatible?

*Having a successful relationship will
depend on the compatibility
of your values and virtues.*

EVEN IN SPITE OF OMINOUS
odds from time to time, the best marriages survive and thrive, and
we know why! They survive and thrive because they are committed
to the core values and virtues present in all great marriages and successful loving relationships.

So, the question of the day is this—does the guy you want to
marry share your values and virtues. Having a successful relationship will depend on the compatibility of your values and virtues.

Let's begin with these values:

1. **The couple in love is committed to always putting
   each other first in their relationship with each other.**

The first thing you notice in all highly successful loving relationships is that those who purport to be in love recognize that their relationship is not about you and me, it is about US. Discovering that YOU are not the center of the universe is the hallmark of a great relationship. Actually putting another human being number one is a powerful indication that you are truly in love.

2. **The couple in love is committed to democracy in their relationship.** Always remember, successful loving relationships are egalitarian. Namely, the best relationships understand that theirs is a shared relationship. If one person has all the power and makes all the decisions, it is NOT love! True love is a very democratic thing!

3. **The couple in love is committed to ensuring their mutual happiness.** Remember, true love is not just about ensuring your happiness. More importantly, and often for the first time in your life, you actually enjoy and are motivated by ensuring the happiness of someone other than yourself. It is a good feeling!

4. **The couple in love values absolute trustworthiness and integrity in their relationship with each other.** If you cannot trust the one you love, then it is not true love! Trust us on that. The most successful loving relationships report that they trust their mate unequivocally and without hesitation. To violate that trust is to undermine and, ultimately destroy, the relationship with the one you say you love.

5. **The couple in love is committed to caring and unconditional love for each other.** When you truly love

someone you do so without conditions. It is not about loving you IF . . . True love is unconditional.

6. **The couple in love is committed to being mutually respectful towards each other.** There is a Golden Rule in true love and it is like the one you learned early in your life, "Do unto others as you would have them do unto you." Do not expect to be treated with respect when you are disrespectful to the one you love. Respectfulness is at the heart of all great loving relationships.

7. **The couple in love values their mutual sense of responsibility for each other.** People in love care for each other in ways that they have never cared for another human being before. They feel a sense of responsibility for another person that they have never felt before. It feels so good to put another's needs above your own. To do so is to love deeply.

The Core Values of all successful loving relationships are at the heart of the matter. If you and your mate master these values, your love could, in all probability, last a lifetime.

But the truth is, there is more involved in successful love and marriage than agreed upon core values. ***The Values are essential, but the Virtues are critical.*** Here's why you can't have one without the other.

This morning, a great friend of ours sent along an article that we were really quite taken with. For those who have read our book, *Building a Love that Lasts,* you may recall a chapter entitled, "A Tribute to Lasting Love" (pp. 259-262). In this chapter we high-lighted the wonderful six-decade marriage of Sandy and Pris, whom we had interviewed for our book.

Over the years, Sandy and Pris have been advocates for "character education" for young people. They have been very philanthropic when it comes to this passion of theirs. (We are sorry to say that Sandy passed away recently.)

As we thought about the article by Dr. Tom Lickona based on his book entitled *Character Matters: How to Help our Children Develop Good Judgment, Integrity, and Other Essential Virtues* (Simon & Schuster, 2004), we were struck by the similarity of the "virtues" he believes essential for "strong character" and the virtues we have discovered in our research over the years about successful loving relationships.

1. **The first essential virtue highlighted by Dr. Lickona is "wisdom."** According to Tom, wisdom is the master virtue that directs all others. Wisdom "tells us how to put the other virtues into practice—when to act, how to act, and how to balance different virtues when they conflict" such as "telling the honest truth" even when it "might hurt someone's feelings." We refer to this notion often in our last book when we speak of the importance of honesty in our relationships with those we love.

2. **The second virtue is justice according to Dr. Lickona.** "Justice means respecting the rights of all persons." In our book, we refer to this virtue as the Golden Rule— mutual love and respect for each other.

3. **The third virtue is "fortitude."** According to Lickona, "fortitude enables us to do what is right in the face of difficulty." Or, more succinctly, doing the "hard right instead of the easy wrong." As we discussed in our book, all successful loving relationships have hard

times, great challenges, and failures. More importantly, however, those whose love lasts a lifetime have
overcome the challenges in life and have been
strengthened by them. Overcoming these challenges
together makes for a stronger and even more loving
relationship. Fortitude is the strength to carry on
even when we find it hard in our relationships to see
the light at the end of the tunnel.

4. **"Self-Control" is the fourth virtue.** In its simplest
   terms, "self-control is the ability and the strength to
   govern ourselves—to control our temper and to regu-
   late our appetites and passions." It is as Lickona says,
   the "power to resist temptation." All marriages and
   loving relationships have their temptations. Trust us
   on that. The successful couples don't act on their
   temptations; hence, they survive and thrive. Read the
   chapter in *Building a Love that Lasts* entitled,
   "Character in Love and Marriage" (pp. 9-11).

5. **The fifth virtue according to Lickona is "love" – "the
   willingness to sacrifice for the sake of another."**
   Successful loving relationships quickly learn that their
   relationship is not about "you" or "me." It is about
   "we" and "us." We write about these notions extensively in our book and blogs. Suffice it to say, people
   who are truly in love do not spend their time finding
   fault with each other—they do not spend their time
   putting down or belittling each other. They find
   strength in the virtues of each other. They love each
   other in the truest sense of the word.

6. **As the purveyors of positive love, we really like
   Lickona's sixth virtue, "positive attitude."** We once

heard a speaker say, "If you frown, you frown alone, but a smile is infectious!" Maintaining a positive attitude is a great virtue. Who wants to be around negative people? Successful loving relationships work like this as well. If your spouse or your lover is always in a negative mood you will work hard not to be around them. The choice of being negative or positive is ours. Choose positive!

7. **Hard work is the "seventh indispensable virtue" according to Lickona.** If you want to be successful in love and life you must work hard. Nothing worth having in a relationship comes easy. You must earn it. Love is something you earn. As we say all the time, the simple things required to make love work take lots of hard work, day in and day out, throughout the life of the loving relationship.

8. **Our favorite virtue is "integrity."** As Lickona says, "Integrity is adhering to moral principle, being faithful to moral conscience, keeping your word, and standing up for what we believe." In love and marriage, you don't cheat on the one you love! You don't lie to the one you love. You are faithful to the one you love. There are no exceptions to this basic virtue. To truly love someone is to tell the truth to them and to yourself.

9. **Dr. Lickona reminds us that "Gratitude is often described as the secret of a happy life."** We would offer that gratitude is the secret of a successful loving relationship. We must show gratitude for the one we purport to love. We should always take the time to thank those we love for their support, their understanding, their sacrifice for us, and for their love. Always

show your gratitude to the one you love. They will love you for it!

10. **And finally, the tenth virtue according to Dr. Lickona is "humility."** Humility "makes us aware of our imperfections and leads us to become a better person." In love and marriage, "humility enables us to take responsibility for our faults and failings (rather than blaming someone else), apologize for them, and seek to make amends." In our opinion, to be truly in love requires us to recognize that we are not the center of the universe—that the world does not revolve around us. People who are truly in love, learn from each other, they respect each other, they value each other, and they recognize that in the best loving relationships, personal humility allows us to understand the simple notion that trying to prove you are right when you are clearly wrong, is not a virtue. Trying to win a senseless and pointless argument is not a virtue. It is good to be humble!

We would encourage you to read more of Dr. Lickona's work and you will see as we do that his "essential virtues" are, in many ways, a mirror of our "seven secrets of a successful marriage."

The truths about the essential values and virtues of successful love and marriage should be self-evident. You and your partner must understand and master them. The success of your love and marriage WILL depend on it!

CHAPTER 10

Does he exhibit financial warning signs?

*Before you decide that this is the right
guy to marry, you need to take a serious
look at how he views financial
goals, choices and commitments.*

*B*ALANCING THE FAMILY
budget requires teamwork. It requires common goals. People in
love support each other through thick and thin—through good and
bad financial times. Before you decide that this is the right guy to
marry, you need to take a serious look out how he views financial
goals, choices and commitments.

People in love don't blame, castigate, or chastise each other
when making financial decisions. They work together to make ends
meet and to prepare for tomorrow. If you can work together to
address head-on the economic challenges in your marriage, your
chances of success get a whole lot better.

The thousands of happily married couples we have interviewed throughout the world all talk about working together to maintain their financial stability. Whether they lost their job, had to take a pay cut to keep their job, were deeply in debt, or faced other financial challenges, they figured out how to roll up their sleeves and work together to solve their problems. Money issues are always discussed, shared and solved together in great marriages.

Since the number one cause of disagreements in a marriage is financially related, **it is critical to observe if any of the twelve financial warning signs are present in the guy you think you want to marry.**

1. **You and your partner are not on the same financial page.** If fact, you and he disagree on almost all financial goals, choices, and commitments.

2. **When you quiz him about his personal financial budget, it is clear he doesn't have one.** When you suggest that budgeting is a good thing and try to show him how to prepare a financial budget, he acts disinterested or he feigns interest and never goes any further with the budgeting process.

3. **Rather than pay off his credit cards each month he pays the minimum, often pays late, or doesn't pay them at all some months.** This is a regular occurrence because he never seems to have enough money to pay his bills.

4. **He is often unemployed and out of work.** He blames others, the high unemployment rate, or circumstances beyond his control for his lack of employment. He often states that it is just a temporary situation, but even when he is working he doesn't seem to keep a job for very long.

5. **He spends his money on a lot of personal toys without regard to the consequences for his personal financial health.** It seems that he is living much beyond his ability to support that level of lifestyle. When he wants something, he buys it without regard to what it costs or how he will pay for it.

6. **The guy you are thinking about marrying tends to be very tight-lipped about his financial situation, rarely ever volunteering information to you.** In longtime successful marriages, they talk about anything and everything. There are no secrets. If he doesn't want to talk about his financial situation, his life goals, or what he thinks about financial matters, that is a red warning flag.

7. **On several occasions since you have been dating he has asked to borrow money from you.** While this isn't in and of itself all that much of a problem, it is another warning sign that should alert you to dig further into his philosophy about financial matters. A man wanting to make a good impression is rarely going to borrow money from a woman he is trying to impress.

8. **You have noticed bills laying on his desk or kitchen table marked "Overdue" or "Past Due."** This is an indication of a serious problem. Credit ratings are easily available with much emphasis on paying bills on time. If bills are laying out openly with overdue or past due marked on them, it indicates a lack of concern for a good credit rating or financial credibility.

9. **He is a grown man, but stills lives in his Mother's house.** While there may be good reasons for this

arrangement, it does throw up a red flag of concern. Is he there to help out his Mother? Is he there because it is easier to live there than go out and earn a real income? Is he there because he can save money to buy his own house? Or??? The reason is important to understand why he is still living with his Mother.

10. **On a scale of 1-10 with 10 high, he ranks a 5 or less when it comes to ambition.** This is a real issue to be totally concerned with. Without ambition, the two of you are going to have a hard time making your marriage work for a lifetime together.

11. **He has been in a college or other training program for such a disproportionately large amount of time, you are beginning to wonder if he will ever graduate.** While it is commendable to gain additional education or training, there is a time for completion and for seeking a real job.

12. **You often end up paying the bill when you go out to dinner, a movie, a concert, or a sporting event.** While in today's culture it is appropriate for the woman to occasionally pay the bill on a date, it is not the usual case. If the guy you think you are in love with has you pay the bill often, it is a red flag. You need to do your homework and investigate further into his financial plans, philosophy, and practices.

The last thing you want to do is marry a deadbeat—a man who doesn't have a financial plan, good financial practices or a financial philosophy that matches yours. If you go ahead and marry him when you don't agree on finances, you will end up with financial difficulties and potentially endless arguments that will jeopardize your marriage.

CHAPTER 11

What do you really know about him?

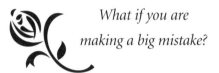

*What if you are
making a big mistake?*

OW WELL DO YOU KNOW
Mr. Right? What if you are making a big mistake? Is he really the
ONE, or should you walk away? These are critical questions you
must ask yourself before you decide whether to move further with
your relationship or whether to decide to walk away to find the real
Mr. Right.

Understanding the following seven signs of trouble can save you
from a heartbreaking relationship:

1. **Actions speak louder than words!** Always remember
   this—it is not what someone says that matters. It is
   how they act. If Mr. Right says one thing and does
   another, beware! If Mr. Right kicks the dog and tells

you how much he loves dogs, beware! If Mr. Right tells you how much he loves you and then disrespects you, beware!

Know this—many people who think they are in love, are often confronted with this reality—Mr. Right does not act like Mr. Right; Mr. Right does not practice what he preaches; and Mr. Right demonstrates in many ways the hypocrisy that guides his behavior. Don't be fooled just because you are in love with being in love.

2. **The Donuts always tell the truth!** You say, what in the world are they talking about? Here it is in a nutshell. You and Mr. Right go to a donut shop to buy donuts. He asks, "What kind of donut would your like?" You say, "I'd like a chocolate covered chocolate and a glazed donut." He brings you a French cruller and a cinnamon covered donut! He takes you to a movie and asks, "What would you like to see?" You say, "The Help or Crazy Stupid Love." He buys tickets for "Rise of the Planet Apes." You get the point. Mr. Right respects you so little he believes that you don't know what you like! Go figure.

3. **He is in the habit of telling you something that isn't quite true.** Your trust in Mr. Right is waning. Your heart (your intuition) is beginning to tell you he is not truthful with you on the things that matter to you. You catch him in lies and distortions, from time to time. He tells you he is going one place and ends up going to another. Mr. Right is starting to make you feel uncomfortable about your relationship with him. He is starting to cause you to question his honesty.

He turns out to be, in the end, someone you could no longer trust. Isn't trust at the heart of all loving relationships?

4. **He is always first in line!** You stop to have lunch at your local fast-food restaurant with Mr. Right. Your mother and father are with you. You arrive at the restaurant. He is first in the door. He does not hold open the door for you and your family to enter the restaurant, and he is the first to order! He is likely to wait for you or your parents to pay for the meal. When the meal is over, he expects you to clean up the mess left at the table. He is the first out of the door. Beware of the warning signs! This is not the man you want to marry!

5. **You do NOT tingle at the presence of Mr. Right anymore**! There was a time in your relationship when he excited you, made you feel special, made you tingle at the sight of him. But now, you find him to be just another ordinary man—a man without feeling, a man without emotion, and a man who no longer excites you or makes you feel special. There is no doubt about this—feeling positive emotion in a relationship is a pre-requisite to a healthy and happy one. When you no longer have intense feelings for Mr. Right, probably time to move on.

6. **Mr. Right turns out to be a fraud!** You trusted him, you loved him, and you thought he was at the center of your universe. Then something happened. He started to disappoint you with his words, deeds, and actions. You could no longer predict his responses, reactions, or the positions he took. He was all over the

board. And in the end, you discovered that he was, indeed, a fraud. He had no moral compass, no convictions, no sense of right and wrong, and no emotional center. You are no longer sure of who he actually is. Frankly, you are beginning to wonder if Mr. Right is really the Mr. Right he pretended to be.

7. **Mr. Right thinks Sex is the most important part of your relationship!** Our research over the years has taught us many lessons about the importance of sex in a relationship. In the early stages of a developing relationship, sex seems very important. But here is the real deal—the successfully married couples we have interviewed in 48 countries on seven of the world's seven continents tell us this—on a scale of 1 to 10, with 10 high, the importance of sex to the overall success of their marriage as 6.2 on a 10-point scale. This finding does not in any way minimize the importance of sex. It does, however, put it all in perspective. It is not the most important part or sole determiner of a healthy and successful relationship. Don't be fooled if Mr. Right tells you that your submissiveness in sex is the most important element to the success of your relationship, you know it is time to move on. Sex is fun, but it does not define a successful marriage or relationship. Take that to the bank.

Mr. Right may not be right for you. You cannot ignore your observations. Sometimes, it takes awhile to discover the truth. However, if you review and understand these seven simple signs of trouble, you will be in a great position to discover if Mr. Right has any of these significant indicators of potential problems.

What if all he wants is SEX?

Men who focus singularly on the importance of sex to the relationship have blown its importance entirely out of proportion to its relevance in a great marriage.

For STARTERS, WE ALL KNOW that good sex can be fun, romantic, exciting, and something that makes most consenting adults feel warm and fuzzy all over. Over the years we have interviewed thousands of successfully married couples, and most report a reasonable degree of satisfaction with their sex life. But here is our most important research finding concerning this issue—no marriage was ever saved or made successful because the couple had a great sex life!

And more importantly, when we ask successfully married couples how important sex is to the overall success of their marriage—to rank on a scale of 1-10 with 10 high—**the average rank**

was only 6.2! This finding has held true in our research for over 30 years. The results are hardly a resounding endorsement for the importance of sex in a successful marriage.

Johnny Cash and June Carter said it best in their famous duet, "We got married in a fever hotter than a pepper's sprout. We've been talkin' 'bout Jackson ever since the fire went out." So, how do successful, happily married couples keep the fire from going out? How do they stoke their fire until it warms everything around them? Marriages change over the years, and in enduring marriages the partners find ways to grow closer together and improve the relationship that once began with the fiery passion of young love and then matured into a lasting love.

You see, marriage is a multi-faceted and highly complex relationship, and in the best marriages no one aspect stands out. The truth is, there are seven pervasive characteristics present in all successful marriages. And guess what, sex is not one of them! Sex is only part of one of the seven characteristics of a successful marriage—the loving touch characteristic. And, much more than sex makes up the characteristic of the loving touch for successfully married couples. Happily married couples touch, they hold, they caress, they kiss, and they gently pat to show affection.

As we say so often in our many interviews and writings, all of the married couples, representing the best marriages we have interviewed, have shared with us the importance of touching in their relationship. One gentleman we interviewed told us that if he passed his wife in the house a hundred times a day, he touched her. To touch someone you love is to acknowledge their presence and to communicate your love for them. That's why the most successfully married couples amongst us touch each other so often.

Men who focus singularly on the importance of sex to the relationship have blown its importance entirely out of proportion to its relevance in a great marriage. Almost as soon as the marriage takes place, the real world issues of finances, chores, health, friendship, support, jobs, future, and much more come into play. While sex provides an intimacy between the two of you, men who are too focused on sex will have difficulty dealing with the realities of life after marriage.

CHAPTER 13

Does he ever bully you?

*Never succumb to a bully
even if he is someone you love deeply,
as to do so diminishes the value of
your relationship, forever.*

*D*ON'T YOU JUST HATE bullies? They try to get what they want by bullying you, by intimidating you, and by making you feel inferior to them. If you are like us, this NEVER works! Yet, so many good women succumb to a bully. And we wonder why?

So what is a bully? In the simplest terms, a bully is someone who can't get what he wants through normal means. What he wants is power. When you deny him that power he resorts to forceful means to get what he wants.

Here is how it works in love and marriage. One of the individuals in the relationship wants something—be it a new car, a new apartment, or a new toy of some variety. The other person involved in the relationship does not. As you might guess, all heck breaks loose!

The "bully" in the relationship must get what he wants. So instead of acting rationally (i.e., Do we have enough money to pay for this?), the bully resorts to name-calling with statements such as, "You are always keeping me from buying things!" or intimidation with statements such as, "If you don't let me buy this I am walking out the door." or they resort to making you feel inferior by saying things like, "How could you be so stupid?"

If you are like most women, you would rather "have peace." So in the interest of maintaining harmony in your relationship, you fall prey to the bullying—you give him what he wants.

But here is the deal—this strategy never works! You give him what he wants and he will then do it to you again! You always succumb to his wishes. You always lose. Letting him win on a regular basis is a bad idea.

The truth is, real loving relationships are not about you and me, they are about US! They are about WE. As we are fond of saying, "It takes two to Tango." You cannot Tango by yourself. Until you learn this important lesson in your relationship, your relationship will be doomed to failure. Finding the courage to stand up to a bully is perhaps the only way to effectively stop the bullying.

If the man you think you are in love with is already bullying you, even before you get married, you need to put a stop to it immediately. If the bullying does not stop, you need to get out of the relationship. The question is, how do you handle the bully in your loving relationship?

The answer in a nutshell is, never succumb to his wishes when he resorts to bullying. Keep your composure. Follow the wisdom of

Rudyard Kipling when he says:

> If you can keep your head when all about you
>
> Are losing theirs and blaming it on you.
>
> If you can trust yourself when all men doubt you,
>
> But make allowance for their doubting too;
>
> If you can wait and not be tired by waiting,
>
> Or being lied about, don't deal in lies,
>
> Or being hated, don't give way to hating,
>
> And yet don't look too good, nor talk too wise:
>
> If you can dream—and not make dreams your master;
>
> If you can think—and not make thoughts your aim;
>
> If you can meet with Triumph and Disaster
>
> And treat those two imposters just the same.

The simple truth is, a bully should never be allowed to win—even if he is your lover. True loving relationships are about making each other stronger and building the self-confidence of each other. True loving relationships are about equality and support for one another.

Once you fall into the trap of intimidation and bullying, your relationship begins its descent into the poverty of relationships. Rarely does a relationship recover from this.

Be strong. Be brave. Stand up for yourself and your ideas and your needs. Never succumb to a bully, even if he is someone you love deeply, as to do so diminishes the value of your relationship, forever.

This is among the most important lessons of love, as well as the lessons of life.

CHAPTER 14

Does he always think he is right?

It is a red flag warning if the guy
you think you are in love with
makes you feel like you
can never do anything right.

WHEN ONE PERSON THINKS
he or she is always right, beware! We have heard from many women
that they are seeking a divorce because they feel they can never do
anything right. It is an issue that needs to be dealt with directly very
early in your relationship and absolutely before you get married.

We had the pleasure recently of responding to personal questions from readers for the Washington Post's on-line marriage
section. One of the readers raised a particularly important question
and we thought the answer would be interesting to women contemplating marriage.

The question from a reader in Washington, D.C. was, "My long-term boyfriend comes from a family of lawyers & arguers. They all pride themselves on being right. I've talked with him & said I find it condescending when he corrects me or says why his way of doing things is better. He is trying very hard to be better about it, but it is really grating on me. What else can I do?"

Our answer to this reader was:

> This is a really important issue, principally because successful communication in a relationship requires mutual respect and understanding. Insisting on being right all the time short circuits or destroys communication and thwarts positive interactions.

> The question we have for you is this, are you confident that he will change that behavior? If he does not, it will grate on your relationship or marriage like a fingernail on a chalkboard. We have heard from many women that they are seeking a divorce because they feel like they can never do anything right.

> This is an issue that cannot be swept under the rug because it will only get worse if you do not deal with it. You need to take the risk of having a very straightforward and honest conversation about this issue with your boyfriend or fiancé. Your satisfaction with his answer will tell you a lot about the future of this relationship.

It is a red flag warning if the guy you think you are in love with makes you feel like you can never do anything right and that he has all of the answers. You need to move on before you commit your life to someone who doesn't encourage and support you.

When we hear longtime happily married women talk about how their husbands make them feel, we hear words like smart, successful, beautiful, accomplished, skillful, talented, capable, and effective. These happily married women also talk about how they were encouraged to achieve higher goals by their husbands. Many say that they would not have been able to be so great without the constant support from their husbands. Never do you hear them say anything about their husbands always needing to be right. Nor do you hear anything about these women feeling like they are always wrong. This is not how it works in successful relationships.

CHAPTER 15

Does he fight fair?

Will he make appropriate compromises, argue fairly and engage in discussions openly with me?

E ARE OFTEN ASKED this question, "Is arguing healthy for a marriage?" The simple answer is, "Yes!" When a husband and wife argue, they are engaging in a perfectly normal and expected part of what it means to be married. In fact, we would argue that disagreement between two people in love is actually healthy for their relationship. To argue or not to argue is NOT the question! The question should be, "How do couples argue effectively and fairly?"

Learning how to fight fair and to make appropriate compromises will go a long way towards keeping a relationship strong. Compromise is rarely ever 50/50. Some days it is 90/10; some days it is 60/40; and some days it really is 50/50. What it isn't is 100/0 or 80/20 with one person getting the advantage all of the time.

The most important question for you is, "Does the guy I am thinking about marrying fight fair?" Will he make appropriate compromises, argue fairly and engage in discussions openly with me?

The truth is, compromise is part of what marriage is all about. Whether it is what to make for dinner, what movie to see, when to have children, where to live or what color to paint the living room, the two of you have to make the decisions together so that both of you can support the decision once it is made. Sometimes argumentation can actually lead to better mutual decisions.

Our interviews with successfully married couples around the world have revealed to us that unilateral decision-making on the part of one partner or the other, more often than not, exacerbates the debate and makes it less likely that a mutually agreeable resolution is possible. In other words, if the guy you think you want to marry makes unilateral decisions and cannot compromise, it will make a marriage difficult at best.

To evaluate your guy's ability to fight fairly use the seven rules of engagement listed below:

1. **When you fight does he fight in a calm manner?**
   That means he doesn't shout or throw things or rant about the situation. That means he thinks about what he is going to say before it actually comes flowing out of his mouth. Does he keep his body language intact or does he take a position of anger or hostility before a single word is even spoken. Does he relax and try to put down the anger he is feeling so he can respond in a calm demeanor or does he immediately demonstrate how mad he is?

2. **When you argue does he refrain from name-calling or shouting ugly verbiage about you?** Do your arguments degrade because he resorts to personal insults. Does he stick with addressing the issues or does he risk doing lasting damage to your relationship with saying hurtful things about you, even if later he says he didn't mean what he said. The problem is that he can't take back his words and that can be extremely difficult when trying to make a relationship last for a lifetime.

3. **He acts like an adult.** He doesn't have temper tantrums during arguments! He doesn't just sit there looking mad without saying anything. He engages in the conversation with the thought of how the two of you solve your problems together as adults.

4. **He keeps the argument logical and focused on the issues at hand.** He doesn't wander off topic to old battles or old scars. Together, you determine what the problem is, what issues need to be dealt with and what are the possible solutions. He is always focused on determining which solution would work best, and keeps your relationship moving towards a positive result, rather than diverting his attention to negative side issues.

5. **He doesn't cast blame.** It never matters to him who is right or wrong. It never matters to him whose fault it is. You share the problems together and stay focused on finding solutions.

6. **He doesn't hold grudges.** As soon as the issue has been resolved, he forgets it and moves on. He doesn't resurrect old arguments in the context of a new one.

He doesn't gloat when he is right and he doesn't remind you constantly about how mad he still is after an argument.

7. **He NEVER let's us separate when we are mad at each other.** We settle our fights before we part, no matter how long it takes. Sometimes, we defer the ultimate decision on an issue until further discussion the next day, but we never leave each other mad at each other! The number one piece of advice given to us by the thousands of happily married couples that we have interviewed over the past 30 years around the world is, "Never go to bed mad at each other."

Remember, it is perfectly okay to argue and debate with the one you love. Better solutions are often arrived at when you engage in wholesome debate. Making sure that the guy you are thinking about marrying knows how to argue fairly and effectively is critically important to a healthy relationship and to a healthy marriage.

CHAPTER 16

Is he really a loser?

Ignoring the warning signs of a loser can come at great risk to your health happiness, and welfare.

SEVERAL YEARS AGO WE came across a wonderful article by Dr. Joseph M. Carver, Ph.D., Psychologist, entitled, "The Loser: Warning Signs You're Dating a Loser"

In our opinion this is one of the best articles on this subject to ever appear in print and on the Internet over the past two decades. It is one of the most wonderful compilations of the "warning signs" of dating a loser you will find and reflects some of the best research on the topic ever written.

Since Dr. Carver's article is so well written, so compelling, and so complete we have decided to highly recommend your reading his original article before getting married. We will simply summarize the important points he makes because we surely could not have written it better.

The list presented below according to Dr. Carver is designed to "provide a manner in which women and men can identify potentially damaging relationships before they are themselves severely damaged emotionally or even physically."

Here is a summary of Dr. Carver's warning signs with our personal commentary, based upon our over 30 years of research on all of the world's seven continents, included in each:

1. **"The Loser will hurt you on purpose."** Walk away from those who do! The hurt they impose on you will be both physical and mental. Their hurt for you will be purposeful.

2. **"The Loser has very shallow emotions and connections with others."** You can't plan your future after three dates! Don't fall for those early statements of "I love you" as they are probably shallow expressions.

3. **"The Loser has a scary temper."** People with bad tempers typically end up turning it on you. Beware!

4. **"The Loser repeatedly puts you down."** They like to chip away at your confidence level by putting you down and correcting you all the time, often in public.

5. **"In order to control someone completely, you must cut off their supportive friends—sometimes even their family."** Once you find yourself isolated and separated from your friends and family, The Loser can control you even more.

6. **"The Loser cycles from mean to sweet and back again."** They will be intentionally mean and hurtful to you one minute and then suddenly sweet and loving the next. These controlling and yo-yo like behaviors will damage your feelings of self-worth and self-esteem.

7. **"The Loser never . . . takes personal responsibility for their behavior."** Losers like to blame you for everything bad that happens and make you think you "had it coming (anger, yelling, assault, aggression)." If this is happening to you, leave this relationship as fast as you can!

8. **"The Loser panics at the idea of breaking up – unless it's totally their idea . . ."** According to Dr. Carver, "Once back in the grasp of The Loser—escape will be three times as difficult the next time."

9. **"The Loser will encourage you to drop your hobbies, interests, and involvement with others."** It is clear that losers want to control you and only want your interests to be theirs!

10. **"The Loser will check up on you and keep track of where you are and who you are with."** The Loser wants to control you, make no mistake about it! They want you to stay home waiting on them. Don't participate in their game.

11. **"In an effort to keep you under control while in public, The Loser will lash out at you, call you names, or say cruel or embarrassing things about you in private or in front of people."** The Loser wants you to keep your opinions and beliefs to yourself. Public embarrassment is how they control you!

12. **"The Loser convinces you that you are never quite good enough."** They want to destroy your self-esteem and convince you that you are lucky you have them because nobody else wants you. Making you feel inadequate is their goal.

13. **"The Loser has a tremendous sense of entitlement . . ." As Dr. Carver says, "This sense of entitlement will be used against you."** Don't let them punish you because they feel entitled to do so.

14. **"The Loser will be jealous and threatened by anyone you are close to . . ."** You will withdraw from your family and friends. Your personality will change. You quit talking about those you are close to in order to avoid his rage and condescension. He will try to convince you that your love is his special love. Don't buy it!

15. **"People define themselves with their stories, much like a culture is described by its folklore and legends."** It is highly important that you listen to the stories they tell you as they will tell "how you will eventually be treated and what's coming your way." Their stories will tell you a lot about their personality. Pay attention!

16. **" . . . the way an individual treats a waitress or other neutral person of the opposite sex is the way they will treat you in six months."** We always say, actions speak louder than words. How he treats the waitress and his dog speaks volumes about him. Pay attention!

17. **"The Loser may have two distinct reputations—a** group of individuals who will give you glowing reports

and a group that will warn you that they are serious trouble." As Dr. Carver says, "If the reputation has two sides, good and bad, your risk is high." If you dislike his friends, be forewarned. He is what his friends are!

18. **"As a relationship with The Loser continues, you will gradually be exposed to verbal intimidation, temper tantrums, lengthy interrogations about trivial matters."** They want you to be alone in life except for them. That way, they can control you. They don't want any interference from others when it comes to controlling you.

19. **"The Loser is so self-involved and self-worshiping that the feelings and opinions of others are considered worthless."** The Loser loves to discount your opinions, as he has no interest in them. They hate to be criticized and will often react with anger "when their behavior is questioned."

20. **"The Loser operates in such a damaging way that you find yourself doing crazy things in self-defense."** Get away from this creep before you suffer permanent psychological damage! You ask family and friends to not bring up certain topics around him. You warn them to be careful what they say around him. You yell and scream a lot when you grow tired of the verbal abuse and his attempts to intimidate you.

When you note any of the aforementioned behaviors in the man you are thinking of marrying, beware! If you notice several, get out of your relationship as soon as possible.

We have learned in over 30 years of research that Dr. Carver has it right—ignoring the warning signs of a loser can come at great risk to your health, happiness, and welfare. Heed the warning signs before it's too late!

CHAPTER 17

Do you talk about serious issues with him?

If the you and the guy you are thinking
about marrying use the seven techniques for
talking about serious issues, you
are well on your way to a
great communicative relationship.

HE "HEART OF THE MATTER" is this—successfully married couples report a high level of satisfaction with the way they communicate with each other, and they attribute their marital success first and foremost to the fact that they have honed their communication skills over time. Oh sure, in the early years even successfully married couples report that they struggled with all this, but over time they got better and better at it because they kept working at it.

So, what are the lessons we have learned from those couples that communicate really well—that communicate effectively on just about every level. As we poured over our many interview notes, seven important themes began to emerge. Review each of these techniques carefully to determine if you and the one you love engage in communication about serious issues using all seven.

1. **Effective communication always begins with proper engagement and in a proper context.** There is a time and place for everything and communicating effectively with each other is no exception. Talking about serious matters cannot occur effectively when dealing with chaos—a blaring television in the background, when both of you have iPhones plugged into your ears, or when you are in different rooms of the house engaging in different activities, where shouting is the only alternative!

2. **There is proper etiquette to follow in effective communication.** Remember, you can't communicate effectively with each other when you are both talking at the same time. It's hard to listen when one or the other is doing all of the talking! You can't hear effectively if you both are shouting at each other. It is always better to lower your voices and speak in a calm manner. Remember, it is never a good idea to blame, accuse, call names, or make nasty remarks. Being ready to communicate and follow these basic rules of engagement will get you off to a good start.

3. **Discussions about serious issues must always begin with agreement about what the issues really are.** Until you work to identify the issue, establish the parameters of the discussion, and agree to solve the

problem or issue together, it is hard, if not impossible, to get your communication with each other up to the level required for proper resolution of the challenge you are confronting. Sometimes the debates and discussions with each other become like two ships passing in the night—they never see, listen, or learn from each other—they are just two ships passing in the night.

4. **A fruitful conversation about important matters always begins with the brainstorming of ideas.** It is important to get your respective ideas out on the table. Talk about the relative strengths and weaknesses of each. Agree on ideas worth exploring. When you agree on a plan, stick to it. When the two of you share the responsibility for the direction or directions you take, you will both feel much more buy-in and commitment, and you will be much more willing to share responsibility for the outcome, good or bad.

5. **The precursor to successful communication is confidence.** Developing the ability to communicate effectively allows for an open and honest expression of opinions and ideas. Being allowed to express a contrary opinion without shouting it out is one of the first signs that you are becoming a confident communicator with your mate. Having you or the one you love disagree with each other's opinions without either getting defensive or unnecessarily argumentative is a clear sign of maturity in your communicative relationship. Successfully married couples tell us they learned these lessons early on and worked on being confident in their expressions everyday. It may start

slow early in your relationship but daily practice builds momentum. When either or both mates lack confidence in their ability to communicate with their spouse, effective communication is greatly hindered.

6. **Never, we repeat, never be judgmental when debating issues with the one you love.** Passing judgment on an idea at the drop of a hat is usually the death of open and honest debate between two people. When you say something like, "That is a stupid idea" or "That is about the dumbest thing I have ever heard," you are putting an arrow through your loved one, and it hurts! When they close down and refuse to further discuss the issue(s) you were debating, then all exchanges end. No solutions are found. And the truth is, the wounds caused by this action further erode the ability of the two of you to engage in healthy exchanges—in healthy debate in the future.

7. **Simple things matter when it comes to discussions about tough or challenging issues.** When serious issues arise and the two of you need to deal with them, there are some simple things that you can do to insure that your exchanges become part of a rational discussion rather than an argument or an endless diatribe about why your mate is wrong. Learn these simple lessons—listen intently to what your guy is saying; make eye contact with him; turn off all electronic appliances (TV, radio, music, iPhone, etc.) so as not to be distracted during your conversation; seek clarification when you don't understand or comprehend something; hold hands when you debate; and never make disagreements personal. Lessons to live by, for sure!

The successfully married couples we have interviewed over the past 30 years report to us that they never felt invalidated by their spouse, that they always felt their arguments were heard, and that their opinions always mattered. If you and the guy you are thinking about marrying can say the same thing and you use the seven techniques for talking about serious issues, you are well on your way to a great communicative relationship.

CHAPTER 18

Is commitment difficult for him?

Many men are afraid to make commitments when it comes to love and marriage!

*F*ALLING IN LOVE IS EASY, but let's face it, many men are afraid to make commitments when it comes to love and marriage! Heck, we live in a disposable world— where it is easy to have "one night stands" and avoid commitment to those we fall in love with, if even for a night.

But you know what—lots of people do fall in love. Lots of people make a commitment to "love through sickness and in health 'til death do us part" and mean it! Most who make this commitment feel honor-bound by the commitments they make! Lots of people fall in love for a lifetime. Honestly, there is nothing unusual about that.

Here is the question of the day—*why do some men find it so difficult to make a commitment to love?*

The thousands of successfully married couples we have interviewed throughout the world have shared many stories with us about their commitment to love. They have described how they formed a commitment to each other—how they decided once and for all how much they loved each other and how they would spend their lives together. While some had trouble with the commitment issue, they found a way to get past it and enter into a fulfilling life-long relationship with the one they love.

So what are the steps along the journey to love and commitment? How do those indecisions about love and commitment manifest themselves in real relationships?

To understand if your guy is having difficulty with commitment, evaluate how he is doing in comparison to the five steps below:

1. **If you wait to make a commitment until you have no doubts, it will never happen.** One of our favorite quotes is by Rollo May. When we were in graduate school studying the field of counseling we got a lot of exposure to him and we love most of what he has written, especially this, "The relationship between commitment and doubt is by no means an antagonistic one. Commitment is healthiest when it is not without doubt but in spite of doubt." Simply stated, if you think there will ever be a moment in a budding relationship when you will say, "I have no doubts about him/her so I am willing to make the lifetime commitment." Well, forget it! Not going to happen. If you wait for that moment to come you will never make the commitment to love anyone for a lifetime.

2. **"Being deeply loved by someone gives you strength, while loving someone deeply gives you courage," said Lao Tzu, a Chinese philosopher.** We think he has it right. It is not enough to be deeply loved, as you must reciprocate profound love as well before a lifetime of commitment can be made. Having strength without courage is much like the cowardly lion in the Wizard of Oz—only when he committed to being courageous could he use his strength effectively. Successful marriage is a lot like that we think.

3. **Friedrich Nietzsche once posited the notion that unhappy marriages are not caused by a lack of love, but by a lack of friendship.** Nothing truer has ever been spoken about successful marriage. You see, the person you commit to must, first and foremost, be your best friend. You cannot make a lifetime commitment to someone you only love. Lifetime commitments are made to those we consider our best friends! When we ask successfully married couples who their best friend is they always say the name of their spouse.

4. **Making a commitment to another human being for a lifetime also requires your resolve to make, an "unalterable decision," as Alfred Adler says.** Adler goes on to say that "... real examples of love and real marriages ... do not allow ... men or women (to) contemplate an escape. In none of the serious and important tasks of life do we arrange such a getaway." Someone who wants a successful marriage cannot promise a lifetime of commitment to someone they purport to love while plotting an escape at the same time. A true commitment is unalterable!

5. **And finally, remember this about commitment—it is NOT an on again, off again proposition.** Commitment to someone whom you love and consider your best friend can't be here today and gone tomorrow. In the best marriages there is a consistency to commitment. Love and friendship can run hot and cold from time to time, but the commitment to the one you love must be an everyday thing. Commitment is forever.

CHAPTER 19

How will you know if he really loves you?

The answer is simpler than you think.
In the end, there are
Seven Tests of True Love.

SINCE TIME IMMEMORIAL, the most important question of the day for women is this, *How will I know if he really loves me?* The answer is simpler than you think. In the end, there are *Seven Tests of True Love.*

As our many readers know, we have been studying successful marriage and relationships for three decades. And frankly, we get asked this question a lot.

Here's the good news – based upon our research we have learned the answer to the question, "How will I know if he really loves me?" **If you pay close attention to the following seven indicators, you will know the answer to this timeless question as well:**

1. **If you observe his actions rather than his words, what have you learned?** Does he talk about how nice he is, yet kicks his dog? Does he talk about respect for you, but jumps to the head of the line when you order lunch or dinner? Does he tell you how much he loves you, but decides for you what you should eat, the drink you should like, the donut you should choose at Dunkin' Donuts, or the movie you should like on Saturday night?

   Here's the truth—actions always speak louder than words! Never, ever, fool yourself into thinking that his actions don't matter. Always remember this simple truism—he is what he does! Ignore this notion at your peril.

2. **Does he always treat you with respect or does he do so** sparingly and inconsistently? People who are truly in love know this—treating the one you love with respect is a full time activity!

   You cannot pick and choose the time and place to be kind, considerate, and respectful. He either is all of these or he is not. He is not allowed to choose the time and place to be one or the other. He is either respectful full-time or he is not. It really is that simple. He is not entitled to pick and choose!

3. **In your relationship, are you relegated to second-class citizenship or are you an equal partner?** When someone really loves you, they treat you as an equal partner—as a person who has an equal voice in your relationship.

   If he makes the significant decisions in your relationship and relegates you to following his directives, then he really does NOT love you. In the best loving relationships between a man and a woman, both share equally in the relationship.

4. **When you are in love, you know this—you cannot imagine life without the one you love!** So try this question on him, "Honey, do you love me more than life itself? Can you imagine life without me?" If his answer is NO to one or both of these questions, he doesn't love you! If his answer makes you wonder about the depth of his commitment to you, he doesn't truly love you.

Here's the deal—someone who truly loves you cannot imagine life without you. We know this to be true from three decades of research on love and relationships. If he suggests otherwise, he is not the man you should commit your life to!

5. **People who love each other tell each so everyday of their lives together.** Does he tell you he loves you? Does he do it without prodding? Does his love for you come naturally, repeatedly, and frequently?

The truth of the matter is this—when you love someone, you tell them. And don't fall for that old line that goes like this, "I don't need to tell her I love her because she knows." This notion is just plain wrong! You need to hear it. If he doesn't tell you, then your relationship has a problem.

6. **One of the underlying notions in the best relationships is this, "I trust him with my life and my sacred honor.** I trust him more that life itself." Your trust in him is unequivocal and without hesitation.

Here is the question of the day—Is the man you purport to love a man you trust without question? If the answer is no, then you need to reconsider the question, does he really love me?

7. **In the end, if he really loves you, he is always there for you—through the good times and the bad.** When somebody loves you, they love you through thick and thin. They love you without conditions. They love you when you are at your best and when you are at your worst.

When you are really in love, he makes you feel good. He makes you excited about where your relationship is going.

The measure of his love for you is always about consistency. When you love someone, you cannot pick and choose the times you show you care, when you express love, and when you demonstrate your affection for the one you love. If his love for you is conditional, sporadic, and only comes when the times are good, you have to answer yourself this simple question—does he really and truly love me? You decide.

In the end, if he really loves you, he will meet the *Seven Tests of True Love*. If he can't pass this test—then you need to reconsider how true his love actually is. If he passes the test, he will have demonstrated how much he really loves you.

BEFORE YOU SAY "I DO"

HOW TO MARRY THE RIGHT GUY

Are you just in love with being in love?

Being IN LOVE is easy
—just like the Cinderella story—
but making love last
takes hard work.

HE CINDERELLA STORY IS a wonderful story. It does, indeed, warm the heart. It certainly inspires. Love is always inspiring! But the truth is, it is an idealized version of falling in love that rarely ever approximates the reality or the truth of what love really means—of what love might mean for a lifetime.

When young women hear the Cinderella story, they want to believe that their prince charming will sweep in with the wind. And for sure, every young man wants to find his Cinderella—someone to put the glass slippers on. But too many people look for this fairy tale version of love. Unfortunately, idealized love and real love are not always the same.

A dashing young man can sweep you off your feet. The spine tingles; the heart races, the face flushes, and the lips tremble. Love has feelings—and IS a feeling!

And here is the truth—being IN LOVE is easy—just like the Cinderella story—but making love last takes hard work. You have to be ready to do the hard work it takes day in and day out of your loving relationship. Being in love with the concept of LOVE will cloud your rational thinking about the reality of what it takes to make a relationship last for a lifetime together.

Here is where Cinderella comes in. Falling in love at the stroke of midnight is easy. Putting on the glass slipper isn't all that hard. But as most of you know, the beginning of love is easy, but the sustaining of love is the difficult part.

Our greatest challenge as folks who have researched successful marriage for more than 30 years is to convince those falling in love that the Cinderella story is only the beginning of love, not the end.

The truth is, the Cinderella version of love rarely ever happens. Somewhere along the way, someone forgot to tell those who think they are in love that life isn't always fair, just, and beautiful all the time. Sometimes, the reality of love and the "Cinderella of love" are not the same. Trust us on this!

There is no doubt—love is grand! Falling in love is amongst the most important things we will ever do in our lifetime. Falling in love and being in love is a wonderful place to be. Make no mistake about that!

But here is where the truth comes in—to fall in love and be in love is not only the creation of an emotional attachment between two human beings, it is the rational connection between two people who choose to love each other for a lifetime. And that is serious business!

Blinding ourselves to the true meaning of love—fooling yourself into thinking that momentary love is real love—is to make the mistake that leads to the abrupt ending of so many marriages.

Being truly in love is not a temporary thing! Letting our emotions dictate our immediate actions when it comes to love and marriage is a mistake. True love comes with time. True love is not a Cinderella story, it is a story of commitment and love for a lifetime. True love transcends time. There is nothing like it if you are ready to accept the hard work it will take to make being in love turn into true love for a lifetime.

What are the 7 things to discuss before marriage?

The critical point is that you need to have confidence that you know the answers to these questions before you make the commitment for a lifetime of marriage with him.

*W*HAT YOU DO IN THE early stages of your relationship will go a long way towards determining the overall success and longevity of your marriage. Our research reveals that there are seven critical issues you need to have honest discussion about before getting married.

Below are the seven critical issues with the questions you need to be able to answer about the guy you are thinking about marrying. These questions are not meant to be a quiz that you give him.

If you are acting like the grand inquisitor, it could be a real turn-off and appear that you do not trust him. However, these questions are important for you to have answers to, but they may not be questions that you ask him directly. Instead, you need to overhear conversations, observe behaviors, see how he interacts with his friends and family, and listen carefully to what he says about each of these issues throughout your many conversations with him. In other words, you need to pay attention, observe carefully. The critical point is that you need to have confidence that you know the answers to these questions before you make the commitment for a lifetime of marriage with him.

1. **Love: Why do you love each other?**

   Starter Questions:

   • Why do you want to marry me?

   • What don't I know about you?

   • Are there things that bother you about me?

2. **Faith: What do you believe in—what is your moral code?**

   Starter Questions:

   • What are your spiritual beliefs?

   • How committed are you to us treating each other with respect?

   • How important is trustworthiness and integrity?

   • What do you see as the advantages of staying married to me?

   • Have you had any past moral issues such as a criminal record, drug abuse, alcohol abuse, physically or mentally abusing another person?

3. **Children: Are children important or unimportant to your marital relationship?**

Starter Questions:

• Do you want to have children?

• If we have children, will one of us stay home with them, and if so, who?

• What experiences have you had with children?

• Do you have a sexually transmitted disease that could effect having children?

• If it will be a blended family, what roles and responsibilities will the step-dad or step-mom assume?

4. **Your Hopes: How do you see the relationship evolving in 5, 10, and 20+ years from now?**

Starter Questions:

• What are your hopes for our marriage in 5 years, 10 years and 20+ years?

• How will our marriage affect your relationship with your friends and family?

• If everything were perfect, what would we be doing together in 20 years?

• What are your goals for your future?

• What are your goals for my future?

5. **Decision-making: How will decisions be made in our marriage?**

Starter Questions:

• How should we make decisions about important issues in our marriage?

• When we disagree, how can we resolve issues amicably?

• How will we collectively handle our financial resources?

• What will be each of our roles and responsibilities with regards to household duties and chores.

6. Your Desires: What do you cherish the most?

Starter Questions:

• If our house was on fire what would be the first thing you would save?

• How important do you think sex will be to the success of our marriage?

• What interests do you feel passionately about?

• What do you want to do most when we have unencumbered time?

7. The Future: Can you imagine life without each other?

Starter Questions:

• What are your dreams for our lives together?

• What do you do to ensure your good health so we can have a long life together?

• Can you imagine a day when we wouldn't be together?

It is clear to us that these seven leading topics of discussion are important predictors of the health and strength of your relationship with each other and, as a consequence, great predictors of the overall success of your marriage.

Based on the responses we have gathered from the best marriages around the world, the answers to these questions will tell you a lot about the viability of your relationship and is a valid predictor of whether or not your marriage will stand the test of time.

Our advice—discuss these seven issues before you get married and listen very carefully to the answers. The answers will give you a clear window to see into the guy you are thinking about marrying.

Will family and friends impact your marriage?

The relationship between husband and wife trumps everything else. It has to come first before friends and other family members.

ANY PUNDITS TALK about the importance of friends, family and childhood experiences to the success of love and marriage. But how important is a sturdy support system of friends and family to couples with highly successful marriages?

Successfully married couples have NOT reported to us that having a sturdy support system of friends and relatives was a prerequisite to their successful marriage. Quite the contrary—the thousands of happily married couples that we interviewed have reported to us that **the strength of their personal relationship with each other was based, well, on their relationship with each other,** irrespective of their friends and relatives! Imagine that! Having friends and a supportive family is nice, but it is certainly NOT a pre-requisite to a blissful, happy, and successful marriage.

Here is another part of that supportive family issue—a stable childhood is NOT a prerequisite to a successful marriage. We have interviewed couples that have been successfully married for 30-77 years and virtually none of them have reported that a **"stable child-hood" was the defining element in their successful marriage.**

In fact, most of the successfully married couples we have inter-viewed suggest to us that their childhood experiences didn't matter much with regard to their marriage. Their marriage depended, more than anything else, on their relationship with each other. The success of their marriage was determined by the strength of their relationship with each other—nothing more, nothing less. Let's leave the blame on childhood experiences—for good or bad—behind as unworthy when it comes to a successful marriage.

What matters most when you are contemplating marriage is that you talk openly about the relationships you both have with your friends and families. You both need to think about how those relationships will change after you get married.

Some of the important issues to be discussed are: will we still go out individually with our drinking buddies or girl friends; will we talk to our parents daily; what type of relationship do we want to have with our mutual friends; and how often will we visit our parents and families. While friends and family are very important, the roles they play in your lives when married will be quite differ-ent.

The relationship between husband and wife trumps everything else. It has to come first before friends and other family members.

As human beings, we have this amazing capacity to love and be loved. In a successful marriage, this notion is multiplied ten-fold! Successful marriage represents an accumulation of the reciprocal notion of loving and being loved by the two people in the relationship.

CHAPTER 23

Does age difference matter?

While love is the most important aspect
of any long-term relationship,
an age difference of more than
ten years can lower your chances
of having a successful marriage.

O VER THE YEARS,
we have been asked if the age differential between people contemplating marriage really matters. Our answer—it depends!

When you are truly in love, your age and the age of the one you love really doesn't matter for the most part. But there is a reality to this notion as well. Sometimes it does matter.

When you are 17, contemplating marriage to someone who is 47, marriage is probably not a good idea. The life experiences of a 17-year old are very, very different from a person who is 47!

There is a plain truth about this. Someone who is 17 is still a child for the most part. A person who is 47 is experienced, probably accomplished to some extent, and, more often than not, has lived through the trials and tribulations of life—and of living. The wide variation in their life experiences does create a real difference in how they relate in their relationship—make no mistake about it.

There is no magic age differential when it comes to love and marriage. It really does depend on the maturity and experience level of those who are in love. With that said, however, our research does indicate that the closer in age two people in love are, the greater their chances of having a long term and successful marriage.

Most marriages are successful when the age difference between two people in love is approximately ten years or less. When the age difference is greater than ten years the "success rate" starts to go down. When the differential is less than 10, the success rate goes up.

So, how do the facts about age difference fit into the overall research finding about love and marriage? Whether it is one year, five years, ten, or more, true love trumps everything else. The question really is more about "How do you know you are in love" versus "How old is the one you love?"

There are, without a doubt, some simple truths about why relationships last—why marriages are successful. Being IN love is far more important than an age difference between two people who purport to love each other.

Here is a recent example of what we are talking about. Mark and Susan are 50 and 38 respectively. Both are divorced. Both experienced really bad marriages. We will just leave it at that.

The good news, Mark and Susan have discovered each other! In fact, they have fallen deeply and unequivocally, in love.

Listening to them describe their love affair is enlightening and uplifting. They are redefining "Date Night!" These two not only love each other, they have learned what it feels like to respect each other, trust each other, be honest with each other (the core value of all successful relationships), and value each other as human beings.

Both Mark and Susan have children from a previous marriage. Both love their children completely. Both are wildly protective of them. And in fact, both would love no one who did not love their children. And good for them!

In the beginning, they were cautious about their age difference. No longer! Now, they are focused on their love for each other. Their respective ages do not matter.

Being in love trumps everything when it comes to love and marriage, irrespective of age or the age differential of those in love. Age is relative. More importantly, age matters far less in a relationship than true love.

And while love is the most important aspect of any long term relationship, there is a generalization you can make from the age difference research we have done—the smaller the difference in age, the greater the chance at lasting love—the greater the chance at having a successful marriage.

There are no magic elixirs when it comes to love but know this, being in love is more important than age. Love is timeless, of that you can be sure. Go be in love, just understand when love is more likely to be successful.

Does stress impact your relationship?

You cannot build a solid lifelong
relationship until you know
how to deal with stress.

*S*TRESS, STRESS, STRESS!!!
We all feel stress at times. It becomes a problem when you are feeling stress most of the time and it impacts your relationship with the guy you love.

If you are feeling a great deal of stress and tension, invest the time to work through the issues causing the stress and establish a more balanced psychological approach to your problems and worries that will eliminate the overwhelming feelings of stress. Before you get married, you need to determine what is causing the stress, how you can avoid those stress-producing situations, and what you need to do to deal with the stress before it interferes with your relationship.

Here are six tips to help you and the guy you love lower your stress levels by working through the underlying stress-producing issues:

1. **If the stress is coming from situations outside of your relationship, determine the root cause of the stress.** Make a list of all of the things you are worried about, when you are feeling the most stress, what type of situations cause you to feel the most stressful, and what life problems you are facing. Just jotting down your thoughts about these issues can either confirm that you have some real problems to resolve or put things in perspective to help you minimize your worries.

   If your issues are real and serious, make a plan to deal with the problems head on. If your worries are just worries and not serious problems, then begin doing some self-talk about the positive aspects of your life whenever you fade into your worry mode. Remember the old "glass is half full" saying. If you focus on thinking about the glass being half full instead of half empty, life looks a lot brighter.

2. **If the stress is coming from your relationship, determine what is causing the stress.** Are you arguing about past relationships? Is there something you or the guy you love is doing or saying that causes the stress? Do you feel unheard or unappreciated? Is there tension with friends or relatives in your relationship? Are you pushing too intently for commitment? Are there money issues? Are there life issues such as health, habits, future plans, sports, or hobbies that bleed over into the relationship? Are you just doing too much and being pulled in too many directions?

These are just a few of the starter questions to open the discussion about what, when, where and why stress is such a part of your relationship. Before you can reduce the stress impacting your relationship, you have to understand what is causing it.

3. **Talk about how stress is impacting your relationship.** After determining if the stress is coming from serious problems or just worries about issues that don't really matter, have a meaningful conversation with the guy you love about what is causing the stress and how it is manifesting itself in your relationship. When you know what is causing the stress and how it is affecting your relationship, the two of you are ready to work out a plan to eliminate the stress, reduce the stressful situations, or at least determine a method of dealing with the stress that will not adversely impact your relationship.

4. **Make a plan for dealing with the stress.** Everyone feels stress. How you deal with those feelings determines the impact the stress will have. Make a list of what helps you let your mind rest from negative thoughts; what helps you relax; what makes you laugh; and what makes you feel light-hearted and happy. Build your psychological balance back by doing a few of those things everyday that lift your spirit. When you begin thinking negative thoughts or worrying or "stressing-out" consciously, think positive thoughts and begin doing one of the things that helps you to relax, laugh or feel happy. Feeling less stress is a habit, just like feeling totally stressed is a habit.

5. **Focus on what really matters.** What are your highest priorities? Stick to them and let other less important things go. If you focus on what really matters to you, it will bring you satisfaction and a feeling of self-worth when you accomplish what you set out to do. Stress is less likely to occur when you are engaged in doing what you think is really important. In other words, if you truly love the guy you are thinking about marrying and he really matters most to you, let go of the other things that are causing you stress. Focus on building a great relationship with him. Give your guy your respect, your understanding, your embrace, your kiss and your time. If on the other hand, your guy is not your highest priority, you need to think about what matters most to you and let go of the relationship if it isn't your highest priority.

6. **Take a time out if the stress is too great.** Rather than continue with a relationship when the stress is too great and you don't seem to be able to reduce it, take a time out to regain your psychological balance. If he really loves you, you can take a short time out and he will understand. Regaining your positive psychological balance is critical to sustaining a lifelong successful marriage. You are not ready to enter into a lifetime commitment of marriage if you do not have your psychological balance well established. Remember, getting to the right you has to come first.

Stress is something most people don't think about, it just comes on suddenly and they don't know why they feel the way they do. Taking a breathe when you are feeling overwhelmed with stress, helps you put things in perspective. Figuring out the what, when, where, why and how stress is impacting you and your relationship is a critical step in letting go of those negative feelings. You cannot build a solid lifelong relationship until you know how to deal with stress from outside sources, stress from within the relationship or stress from worrying about things that may never happen.

Are the two of you financially compatibility?

*Since the number one cause
of disagreements in marriage is financial,
it is critical to talk about the
financial issues and come to a solid
agreement before you get married.*

BEFORE YOU DECIDE
that this is the right guy to marry, you need to take a serious look at
how he views financial goals, choices and commitments. Having
compatible financial habits and views can help the two of you avoid
difficult financial arguments later after you get married. If you can
work together to address head-on the economic challenges in your
marriage, your chances of success get a whole lot better.

Since the number one cause of disagreements in marriage is financial, it is critical to talk about the financial issues and come to a solid agreement before you get married.   Difficult unresolved financial issues can destroy a marriage. So, it is very important to invest the time to review together your entire financial status and future goals. In this activity, you will be able to begin that process.

Financial Issues to Discuss:

1. Have the two of you discussed what the limit is for a "major purchase?" In other words, what is the dollar limit you have placed for making purchases without discussing the purchase with each other? Is it $50? $200? $500?

2. Does your strategy for making a "major purchase" include talking it over completely and then sleeping on it before doing so?

3. Have you decided that you will regularly discuss the status of your finances?

4. Have the two of you agreed to have a single checking account to share?

5. Do you openly discuss with each other your financial situation? Are you honest with each other when discussing your finances or do you hold back certain information?

6. Have you established the "credit card rules" (credit limits, purchase amounts, monthly payment schedule, paying your bills on time, etc.) that will apply to your financial relationship?

7. Have the two of you prepared a monthly budget? Do you both know where your money is going? How it is

being spent? Have you taken into account your monthly income, regular bills and an amount for unexpected financial obligations?

8. Have you agreed that your bill-paying activity is a shared responsibility between the two of you?

9. Will you own all major assets jointly? In other words, will both of your names be listed on the car titles and all other major assets?

10. Have you agreed that the two of you will have a monthly conversation about your expenses and financial status?

11. Have you discussed your financial goals for one year, five years and ten years in the future?

12. Do either of you have outstanding credit card debt or any other type of debt? If you do, have you talked about and decided how it will get paid off? Can you reasonably manage your outstanding credit card debt?

13. Have you agreed to put your credit cards in both of your names after you get married?

14. Do you both understand finances, know how to talk to each other about money issues, and have an equal status in making decisions about money?

15. Have you talked about any issues in Chapter 10 that indicate your guy may have a financial warning sign?

If you answered "no" to any of these fifteen questions please take the time to fully discuss them together. Gaining consensus on these questions will facilitate financial stability in your upcoming marriage.

Remember, money is the number one cause of arguments in a marriage. Balancing the family budget requires teamwork. It requires common goals. People in love support each other through thick and thin—through good and bad financial times. If the two of you can gain agreement on these critical financial issues before you say "I Do" your chances for a successful marriage are greatly enhanced.

What words are used in
great relationships?

*The words and phrases you use
tell a lot about your relationship.*

URING OUR RECENT SWING
through the Miami area to interview successfully married couples,
we were asked the question, "Are there words or phrases you listen
for when you interview the best marriages around the world?" We
choose to answer it based on our discovery of how the best marriages are described in our research.

The most successfully married couples (longevity plus measured
happiness according to our marriage interview protocol) use specif-
ic words and phases as they talk about their relationship with each
other. Here is the important lesson for you—if you and the guy you
love do not routinely use these words and phrases in your relation-

ship, you need to take a long, hard look at where your relationship is and where it is going.

Here we go, the words and descriptors used by couples with the best marriages:

1. **Togetherness:** In successful marriages, two become one in so many positive and important ways without losing their individual identities. The best marriages have discovered that it is not about you and me, it is about us, our, and we! It is not about "I" and "me," and "yours." The most important seven words and phases used within this context by successfully married couples are: *We, us, our, together, we are a team, we are like one, we cannot imagine life without each other.*

2. **Truthfulness:** In successful marriages, couples talk about anything and everything. There are no sacred cows—no secrets. In the best marriages you hear these words and phases: *Truthfulness, confidant, we never worry about betrayal, we know nearly everything about each other, we are the keepers of each other's deepest and darkest secrets, we trust each other with our respective lives and sacred honor.*

3. **Respect:** In successful marriages, couples understand that you do unto others as you would have them do unto you. Successful love and marriage is about mutual love and respect. In the best marriages you hear these six words and phrases the most when it comes to respect: *Mutual respect, admiration, we repeatedly engage in acts of kindness towards each other; we do nice things for each other with no expectation of something in return; we attend to each other's needs and*

wants; we say thank you and please; we open doors for each other. Successfully married couples do all these things automatically, without ever thinking about it. They are habitual.

4. **Fitness:** In successful marriages, couples understand that taking care of yourself in a health sense is not sufficient. You must also promote health in your spouse. To live until "death do us part" requires a mutual concern about good health. Here are the words and phrases they use: *Health, fitness, exercise, vitamins, salads, taking annual physical exams on the same day; we worry about what each other eats; we remind each other to "take your medicine;" we take long walks and exercise together; whenever possible we shop for food together!*

5. **Joint Finances:** In successful marriage, it is not YOUR money and MY money. It is OUR money. Here are the words and phrases they use: *Our financial goals, joint finances (no separate checking accounts), joint decision making, we talk before we buy big items, our house, our bills, we look for bargains, and we live within our means.*

6. **Tactile Communication:** In successful marriages, touching each other multiple times per day is the norm. Their mantra is, "I love you so much I must touch you." The best married couples cannot keep their hands off each other! And that's a good thing. They tell us that: *We love to hug; we have great sex when the time is right for us; our hands will always find each other wherever we are; we touch each other often in a day; touching acknowledges the presence of each other*

and reminds us of our love for each other; our hands communicate private and loving messages to each other—it is our private Morse Code. Touching communicates warmth, caring, friendship, love, and understanding.

7. **Surprise:** In the most successful marriages, love is characterized by the notions of variety and spice. Successful marriages are exciting, never boring, and full of unpredictable things. Don't always do that which is predictable. Upend expectancies. Variety is the spice of life! The best marriages use words and phrases like: *Fun; adventure; surprise; romance; always finding something to do together; we never get bored with each other; we are each other's best friends; we do our best to keep our romance alive even during trying or challenging times; we are passionate about each other; we are each other's best company.* In the best marriages, boredom is not an option!

You see, the words and phrases you use tell a lot about your relationship. If you don't hear these words and phrases in your relationship, it is clear you have some work to do. Get started today before it's too late to form the habits that communicate love. Making a lifelong commitment to the guy you think you love without having these words and phrases as part of your everyday vocabulary could be a mistake.

In love and marriage, simple words and phrases mean a lot!

CHAPTER 2 7

Are pre-nuptial agreements necessary?

Caring deeply for someone—loving someone—
is only as real as the honesty of the
relationship between the two people who
profess to love and care for each other.

*W*E HAVE SAID IT BEFORE and we now say it again—the divorce rate in the United States of America is **NOT 50%!** It is more likely, closer to 40%, perhaps, slightly less, according to some estimates. Here are the facts.

According to Brad Wilcox in "The Evolution of Divorce" in the Fall 2009 issue of *National Affairs,* "The divorce rate fell from a historic high of 22.6 divorces per 1,000 married women in 1980 to 17.5 in 2007. In real terms, this means that slightly more than 40% of contemporary first marriages are likely to end in divorce, down from approximately 50% in 1980. Perhaps even more important, recent declines in divorce suggest that a clear majority of children who are now born to married couples will grow up with their married mothers and fathers."

This number clearly approximates what we have been espousing for several years. The clear fact of the matter is this—the divorce rate in America has been going DOWN for nearly 30 years!

What is worse is that many use the inaccurate 50% divorce rate notion to push for pre-nuptial agreements. They argue that since so many people get divorced, signing a pre-nuptial agreement is only prudent and sensible. It is insurance against a failed relationship according to them.

To us, this is like saying, "Let's never get married because our chances of failure are 40% out of 100%." Or, "Let's not fall in love at all because we might fall out of love in the future." Pretty silly, huh?

We believe that Pre-Nuptial Agreements are a bad idea for the most part! Just imagine, telling someone that you love him, but you don't trust him! To us, this is analogous to having two separate checking accounts in a marriage—one for him and one for her. In both cases it becomes a case of yours and mine. Or, how about this, "I love you with the following conditions." Whatever happened to US and WE and love without conditions?

Frankly, we don't believe that the true meaning of "marriage" allows for this sort of duplicitous relationship between two people who purport to love each other. True love means true love—without conditions! You can't have a bona fide loving and successful marriage or relationship when you have a pre-nuptial agreement! People who invented this concept don't know anything about real love and real relationships. Only people with an agenda (often financial instead of loving) would encourage something so anti-love, so anti-relationship, and so anti-marriage.

The sad news—in the United States, prenuptial agreements are recognized in all fifty states and the District of Columbia. This is a sad commentary on the state of love, marriage, and relationships in America. Why do we need them? What ever happened to pure, unconditional love! We believe it still exists! It is still the norm, thank goodness!

According to Wikipedia, "There are two types of prenuptial agreements: a *marriage contract* for people who are married or about to be married, and a *cohabitation agreement* for unmarried couples. A variation for people who are already married is a *post-nuptial agreement.*" We think all three are bad for love, bad for relationships, and bad for marriage. Here's why.

In our research with successfully married couples for over 30 years in 48 countries of the world, we have found a number of recurring and pervasive themes. Foremost among them is an abiding trust in and for each other. They trust each other complete-ly and without conditions. People who truly love each other do so without conditions. They have unconditional love—as it should be.

Like most things in successful relationships, the little things matter. Caring deeply for someone—loving someone—is only as real as the honesty of the relationship between the two people who profess to love and care for each other.

We ask you these critical questions: Do you truly and deeply love him? Do you care for him more that you care for yourself? Is he the one in your life that you would die for? Is he the one you would like to spend the rest of your life on Earth with? Is he the one you share your deepest and darkest secrets with? Is he the one that you cannot imagine life without?

If you answered yes to all of the questions above and he feels the same way, then you are completely and wonderfully in love. People like you do not need a pre-nuptial agreement. What you do need to do is spend your lives together. What you do need to do is cement your relationship with each other. What you do need to do is all of the simple things required to make your marriage or relationship work. What you **don't** need to do is sign a pre-nuptial agreement! Let love reign!

One final note—there are exceptions to our recommendations about pre-nuptial agreements due to very practical reasons and individual nuances. While we believe that pre-nuptial agreements are a bad idea for first marriages, under certain circumstances they may be okay for second or third or fourth marriages. If you have a failed marriage at least once, then you have a much greater chance of getting divorced the next time around. In fact, for second marriages the divorce rate is 67% and for third marriages a whopping 75%.

Therefore, you are far better off to set up the conditions necessary to get out of the marriage without incurring thousands of dollars in legal fees and others costs. Establishing a pre-nuptial agreement before marrying for a second, third, or fourth time will greatly reduce the turmoil and costs involved in a divorce should one occur.

CHAPTER 28

Are you ready to get married?

In fact, there are 15 predictors
of a successful marriage that can
help you decide if you
are ready to get married.

THIS MORNING WE HAD a delightful radio interview with a New York radio station about our research on successful marriage. It is always a pleasure to share the "secrets" of successful marriage with our interviewer and his or her audience. Sometimes we answer questions from the listeners, sometimes just from the host of the show, and at times from both. In this business, you learn pretty quickly to talk on your feet as the questions often come rapid-fire, many of them are questions you've never heard before, and the time to answer them is usually quite short.

We were thrown a question on this radio show that we have gotten before in some form or another, but not as directly or succinctly as the host asked it. His question was, "When am I ready to get married?"

The truth is, this could not be a more important issue to consider as you begin to think about getting married. In fact, there are 15 predictors of a successful marriage that can help you decide if you are ready to get married. If you match these indicators that predict you will have a successful marriage and you feel good about your answers to the series of questions in this chapter, you are ready to get married.

The 15 Predictors of a Successful Marriage

In our speeches, blogs, and world travels we are often asked, "Are there ways to ensure that a marriage will succeed?" The answer is of course, **"no."** Life, love, and marriage do not come with absolute guarantees. Marriage does not come with a warranty.

Let us hasten to add, however, you can greatly increase the odds that your marriage will last a lifetime if your profile closely resembles the following 15 findings we have gleaned from our own research and the marriage research of others whose research we highly value.

If your **"marriage profile"** looks like this, you are well on your way being ready for a lifetime commitment to marriage. These are, in essence, the **"predictors of a successful marriage."**

1. **It stands to reason that you must first pass the *Marry the Right Guy Quiz.*** If you can't get out of the starting

gate with marrying the right guy, the rest doesn't matter. Take the Quiz and if you receive a score of 90 or higher, you have met the first pre-requisite of being ready to get married—finding the right guy to marry.

2. **Wait until you are at least 25+ to get married.** Couples who get married after the age of 25 are far more likely to stay married than those who get married sooner. Doing so will pay many dividends over the years ahead. Experience and wisdom that comes with age will certainly contribute to the success of a marriage.

3. **Have an income-producing job with stability before you get married.** Here's what we know, couples with annual incomes over $50,000 (vs. under $25,000) experience a drastically reduced risk of divorce. Couples who have steady jobs with steady incomes are far more likely to have a successful marriage. Do you and the guy you are thinking about marrying have stable income-producing jobs? Are you financially independent so that each of you can stand on your own?

4. **Do NOT have children in the first year of your marriage.** Bring children into the world when your marriage is ready for them. Nora Ephron once said, "Having children is like throwing a hand grenade into a marriage!" Children are wonderful, but they bring stress and challenges to a marital relationship, especially to a new marriage. Have children when you know and understand each other and your marriage is ready for the responsibilities associated with parenting. Your marriage will be well served, make no

mistake about that. Are you talking about getting pregnant right away? Have you had the discussion about children and when you want to have them? Have you taken steps to insure that you don't get pregnant before marriage or early in your marriage?

5. **Being spiritual and/or religious is good for your marriage.** Couples that consider themselves religious or spiritual (vs. not) are considerably less likely to get divorced. Faith and spirituality contribute to the sense of oneness felt by successfully married couples—a necessary prerequisite to a long and happy marriage. Have you openly discussed spirituality and religious beliefs with the guy you are thinking about marrying? Do you have similar views? Can you accept each other's differences? Have you talked about how you will raise your children—in what faith or spiritual upbringing?

6. **Focus on getting an education that includes post-secondary training (college, trade school, etc.).** College educated couples have a much less chance of divorce than those with only a high school diploma. Education almost always leads to enlightenment and understanding and more tolerance for the views of others—so critically important in successful marriages. In fact, college educated women are more likely to get married than their less educated counterparts, and much more likely to have a successful marriage. Have you discussed with the guy you love what he thinks about your educational goals? Have you discussed what his goals are? Have you discussed how you will achieve those goals?

7. **Make sure the guy you love is your best friend.** When someone asks you who your best friend is, the honest answer **must be**, "The guy I want to marry." There is no other acceptable answer to this question. If you answer this question correctly, your marriage has a better than average chance of success. Being in love is never enough without friendship. All long-term successfully married couples know this to be a fact!

8. **Always fight fair in your relationship.** All married couples argue—the good, the bad, and the ugly marriages—they all do it. The difference is **how** they argue. If you decide to submerge your feelings, let the anger fester, and go to bed mad at each other—well, you are heading down a path that could ultimately lead to the destruction of your marriage. Arguing is healthy for a marriage. Just fight fair and never make your arguments personal and hurtful! Do you and the guy you love fight fair with each other? Do you always feel respected when you are arguing?

9. **Never lose your individual identity or subjugate your individual strengths just because you got married.** While in many ways "two becomes one" in the best marriages, losing your own identity is not a pre-requisite to being happily and blissfully married. Quite the contrary, losing the sense of "who you are" will hurt your marriage. It will not help your marriage. Be true to your identity as a human being. If you feel you are losing your individual identity because of your relationship with the guy you are in love with, stop and take a good hard look at what is happening.

10.**Never, we repeat, never engage in acts of infidelity.**
While some marriages survive infidelity, the **overwhelming majority** do not. Think long and hard
about what you will lose before you engage in infidelity—before you violate the most sacred of marital
trusts. If the guy you are in love with has engaged in
acts of infidelity while you were engaged, you need to
think about his basic characteristics. Will he continue
that type of deception after you get married?
Infidelity requires lying and cheating. It breaks down
any level of trust the two of you have.

11.**Always allow time to be alone—for both of you.** We
have learned over the past three decades of research
one fundamental truism—every human being has a
fundamental predisposition to be alone, to be by
themselves from time to time. Allowing yourself time
to be alone to your thoughts each day will serve you
and your marriage well. Extending the same opportunity to your spouse will pay huge dividends for your
marriage. A couple that does not follow this simple
advice could place their marriage in grave jeopardy.
Does the guy you are thinking about marrying give
you a chance to think for yourself? Does he allow you
time to be alone or do you feel smothered? Does he
respect your desire to have quiet time?

12.**Talk about anything and everything!** Marriages
thrive on open communication and honest discussion. The most successfully married couples we have
interviewed around the world tell us that they have
learned to communicate frequently, fairly, openly, and
honestly.   Mum is NOT the word in marriages that

work! Practicing communication with your spouse each and every day is a necessary prerequisite for the success of your marriage. There should be no sacred cows in your marriage! Does the guy you are thinking about marrying engage in open and honest communication with you? Does the guy you are thinking about marrying want to talk about anything and everything with you?

13. **Always show mutual respect and admiration for each other.** The best marriages repeatedly engage in acts of kindness towards each other. They do nice things for each other with no expectation of something in return. They work hard to understand each other's needs and wants. They say thank you and please. They open doors for each other. Successfully married couples do all these things automatically, without ever thinking about it. But remember—these behaviors take daily practice! Do you see these behaviors in the guy you love? Does he always remember to be respectful and treat you with kindness and admiration? Do you feel that you naturally respect and admire him?

14. **The greatest joy in life for successfully married couples is spending time with each other.** If you do not feel this way, you do NOT fit the profile of the most happily and successfully married couples we have interviewed around the world. Couples who love each other deeply, who want to spend their lives with each other, and who cannot imagine life without each other, will almost always tell you this—the one they want to be with more than anyone else is their spouse. There is no substitute for togetherness when it comes

to a happily married couple, make no mistake about that. This is not a feeling gained after marriage. This is a feeling you have to have before you commit to a lifetime of marriage with the guy you love.

15. **Understand that all marriages go through seasons - much like the seasons of nature.** A marriage is born in the spring, blossoms over the summer, grows to maturity in the fall, and settles in over the winter. When we find true love, most of us find it for a lifetime. Those marriages and relationships that last over time started with the simple planting of a seed. The seed was nourished over time. Love grown with tender and loving care matures into fully-grown love that can withstand the tests of time. You can make your love and your marriage last for a lifetime with the right start and nurturing it along the way.

There is a profile for marital success—there are predictors associated with the best marriages and they do not occur by accident or happenstance. It takes hard work to make a marriage work.

There are characteristics associated with success and telltale signs of impending failure. Match these characteristics and the odds are in your favor of having a successful marriage. Ignore the predictors and do so at your own peril. The choice is yours.

Questions to ask yourself before deciding if you are ready to get married:

1. **Do you both want the same things?** What are your goals? Do your goals match his goals? Can you work like a team to achieve those goals?

2. **Do you want to change him?** Thinking about everything you know about him, are there things he does or

things about him that you would like to change?
While you don't have to love everything about him,
you have to be willing to accept him just as he is.
Wanting to change him never works. Remember,
there is one truism you can take to the bank—you
cannot change him! Either accept him the way he is—
warts and all—or move on.

3. **When you have problems, do you work together to
   solve them?** Teamwork is the hallmark of a great marriage. If you are not already working together as a
   team to solve problems or resolve issues before you get
   married, it will be difficult to learn how to do that
   after marriage.

4. **Are your lifestyles compatible?** Can you live together?
   Do one of you like country living and the other city
   living? Is one of you laid back and the other high
   strung? Does one of you like traveling and the other
   one is content staying around the house? Do you both
   love the arts? Do you both love to curl up by the fire-
   place and read a good book?

5. **Do you believe in each other?** Do you believe that the
   one you love is capable of great things? Do you think
   the one you love will be better if he is with you? Do
   you feel that you are a better person when you are with
   him?

6. **Do both of you have basic living skills?** Can you both
   live on your own? Can both of you cook, pay bills,
   balance a budget, and do basic maintenance jobs?

7. **Do you care about each other's needs?** Can you put
   each other's needs first? Do you worry about each

other's happiness and success? Do you think you can help each other be successful?

8. **Are you sure about each other?** Do you really love each other? Do either of you still have doubts? If you do, figure out why. Dig deep into your respective thoughts and analyze what is worrying the two of you or what you are not sure about. Determine if your worries are valid. If so, have an open discussion with each other about the issues. If you still have doubts, find a trusted person or counselor to talk with about it. Before you get married for a lifetime, BE SURE!

When you are contemplating marriage you should start to pay very close attention to the one you think you love. Remember, actions and deeds trump words every time! Watch very carefully his actions and make sure that they match his words. Does he do the simple things day in and day out, or not? Simple things matter, and the simple truth is if you do not see the behaviors you want and expect from the one you are thinking of marrying, it will only get worse over time.

Deciding if you are ready to get married begins with love. Agreement on the "core values" of marriage will grow the love, and doing the simple things day in and day out will sustain the love.

SIMPLE THINGS MATTER TO
SUSTAIN A RELATIONSHIP

HOW TO MARRY THE RIGHT GUY

CHAPTER 29

Simple things matter in your relationship

It is an established fact—successful love is based on an accumulation of having done the simple things.

NO LOVE HAS BLOSSOMED or been sustained without doing the "simple things." Big things don't matter until your relationship has mastered the art of doing the simple things day in and day out in your relationship with the guy you want to marry.

All too often in life, people make assumptions about love and relationships that do not stand up under scrutiny—that are not supported by the available evidence. So, what are the facts?

One of the great misconceptions of all time about love and relationships is this—just do the big things and everything will turn out well. And what do the big things include? For starters the list includes "having financial stability in your relationship," "being in love is all that matters," "having a good job and a house in the suburbs," and so it goes. But the truth is, these big things are important, but they are only by-products of doing the simple things. Here's what we mean.

It is an established fact—successful love is based on an accumulation of having done the simple things. If you want your marriage and your relationship to succeed, just do the simple things! Do them day in and day out. When your relationship has mastered the "simple things" you have a chance to make it work. You have a chance to make it last. But if you don't, well, failure is an option.

There is another important fact of life when it comes to love and relationships—there will be big challenges to address in your relationships, of that you can be sure. You might have to deal with financial setbacks, serious illness, the loss of a job, or the death of a loved one. And trust us on this—if your relationship with the one you love has mastered the art of doing the simple things day in and day out, the likelihood of your relationship making it through the tough times are multiplied many times over.

So what are these simple things? Here is a list of 50 examples of the simple things that matter to get you started. Don't wait—start today doing as many of the simple things as you can and then start your own list of simple things you can do to make your love last forever.

1. Take long walks together.

2. Snuggle in the morning before you get out of bed.

3. Recognize kindness with a thank you.

4. Call when you are going to be late.

5. Share a good bottle of wine while watching a sunset.

6. Be generous with your time for each other.

7. Compliment your lover about something he did today that made him special.

8. Hold hands often.

9. Bring home flowers for him when it is not a special occasion.

10. Leave a sticky note on your lover's wallet or purse telling him to come home safely to you because you love him.

11. Ask him about his dreams and his dreams for your future together.

12. Open doors for each other.

13. Take a bike ride together, bringing a picnic lunch for a secluded spot along the way.

14. Walk your dog together.

15. Fix your lover breakfast in bed for no special reason.

16. Say "I love you" several times during each day.

17. Treat your lover with courtesy at all times.

18. Help clean off the table and do the dishes after dinner.

19. Compliment your lover's cooking.

20. Tell him one reason why he means so much to you.

21. Take him to his favorite restaurant in the middle of the week.

22. Lovingly touch your mate 100 times a day.

23. Surprise him by bringing him lunch when he least expects it.

24. Prepare meals together as often as you can.

25. Spend an evening listening to music and making a CD or playlist of your favorite songs together.

26. Never let things get stale. Upend expectancies and delight your lover.

27. Always point out the positive attributes of your lover, both at home and in public.

28. Give him a massage or a back rub.

29. Look directly into your lover's eye when you are having a conversation.

30. Be his best cheerleader for his accomplishments.

31. Plan a bubble bath together and see where it leads.

32. Go dancing together.

33. Talk about everything. No topic is too small or too big. There are no sacred cows.

34. Always demonstrate respect for each other in your words and in your actions.

35. Schedule your annual physicals on the same day.

36. Plan a week of healthy meals together with foods that you both enjoy.

37. Write him a love letter and leave it for him to find in the morning.

38. Sit down and go over the finances together before you pay the bills for the month.

39. Take your lover to a movie, putting your arm around them like you used to when you were first dating.

40. Write personal Valentine's Day cards.

41. Turn off the television and talk to each other.

42. Go for a boat ride, car ride or train ride that isn't planned and doesn't have an itinerary.

43. Sing a song together and to each other.

44. Go to Disneyland—just the two of you.

45. Plant flowers together.

46. Share a tuna melt.

47. Kiss each other passionately.

48. Go to the zoo together.

49. Engage in simple acts of kindness daily.

50. Sit in your porch swing and gaze at the stars.

The point is, simple things matter and when you practice doing them, they accumulate. Simple acts of kindness add up. And always remember, you can't keep turning on then turning off doing the simple things. You have to consistently engage in doing the simple things day in and day out. When you do, you will be surprised at how well this simple notion works. Start engaging in them today so you can get into the habit even before your wedding.

CHAPTER 30

The 5 things you should say to him everyday

*All couples at times get themselves
in a negative cycle that needs
an immediate injection
of positive communication.*

*N*EGATIVISM CAN EASILY
creep into even the best relationships, causing a pattern of negative
actions and thoughts that can overpower the relationship. The
question often asked by couples is "How can we create positive
interactions with each other on a daily basis so negativism doesn't
take hold of our relationship?"

From time to time, all relationships get themselves in a negative
cycle that needs an immediate injection of positive communication.

Couples at times forget to focus on the positive elements of their relationship with each other, and often try small intermittent positive actions that usually do not provide a foundation for lasting positive communication.

Over the years we have heard advice from thousands of happily married couples regarding the important things you should say to your spouse everyday. These couples communicate effectively on just about every level and have learned how to build positive interactions with each other on a daily basis. As we studied our mountains of interview notes, important lessons emerged.

Here are their recommendations for the five things that you should say to the one you love each day to build positive interactions:

1. **I love you.** These are the three favorite words of every lover. It is a simple, direct, powerful, and highly meaningful statement. And don't fall into the trap of so many couples that say, "Oh, I don't need to tell him I love him. He knows I do." Not true! You still must still tell the one you love multiple times each and every day that you love them.

2. **I am so lucky to be with you!** If you want to touch the heartstrings of the one you love, tell him this. Just imagine being reminded every day that you are a blessing to the one you share your life with.

3. **You look terrific today!** There is a major truth we have learned over the years—successfully married couples really do find each other attractive. And you know why—because they look for the most positive characteristics in each other in both a physical as well as a

psychological sense. Telling each other this daily is a powerful statement of love.

4. **I would like your opinion and value our wisdom.** Successfully married couples have great admiration and respect for each other. They value each other's opinion. Their most trusted advisor in life is their spouse. Asking for your loved one's opinion about issues and acknowledging his wisdom builds a strong bond between the two of you.

And finally, every day of your life with the one you love, point out one of his strengths. Try this, "Sweetheart, did I ever tell you how much I admire the positive way you treat others?" Or, "Honey, you have such a wonderful way of handling tough situations!" Make sure the strength you highlight is a true strength.

Each and every day, highlight one or more of your soulmate's most positive virtues. Build a foundation of positive interactions with the guy your want to marry by remembering to say these five things every day.

The 5 things you should NEVER say to him

One negative or hurtful statement can
undo an entire day's positive actions and
words, damaging the very
core of the relationship.

J
UST AS IMPORTANT AS
saying the right thing to the one you love is to avoid saying statements that have the potential to destroy the foundation of the
relationship. Saying just one wrong thing can negate an entire day
of good statements and actions. Negative and hurtful statements
can have the power to cut through the very fabric of the bond
between two people in love.

Here are those five things you should NEVER say to the guy you love:

1. **It's your fault!** Sometimes, a financial decision goes bad, you don't meet up at the right time for a commitment, or some household calamity occurs. And know this—things do go bad from time to time in any relationship. Decisions turn out wrong. Stuff happens! But the blame game never works! It alienates. It divides. It most certainly undermines trust and openness in your relationship.

2. **I told you so!** Trust us on this—these four words are rarely ever used in successful relationships. This kind of "comeuppance" has no place in a loving relationship. There is no need to remind your loved one that you were right about something and he was wrong. Talk about wasted criticism!

3. **Saying "I am upset with you about this or that . . ." in a public setting.** Telling private secrets or criticizing the guy you are thinking about marrying in public or to someone else can do permanent damage to the trust in your relationship. True or not—it doesn't matter. Keep private things private.

4. **Why do you always . . .** Focusing on your loved one's weaknesses rather than building on his strengths will only increase his weaknesses and diminish his strengths. This habit can send a relationship into a downward spiral if weaknesses are pointed out and commented upon. Success does breed success. Stick with the strengths and don't focus on weakness.

5. **Ask for your loved one's opinion and then do the opposite.** We have heard from many angry divorced or almost divorced couples that this is the greatest indicator of "disrespect." If you ask where the guy you love wants to go to dinner and he suggests a couple of places, then you select a different one, by your actions you said, "I do not respect your opinion and don't care what you think!"

Since saying negative or hurtful things can be damaging to a loving relationship, it is wise to take extra caution before engaging your mouth when these negative thoughts come into your mind.

Here are some quick tips to help you THINK BEFORE YOU SPEAK!

1. **Will my comment hurt?** Sometimes we just blurt out things that are hurtful or negative without thinking about their impact. Use the old count to five rule before you open your mouth with a negative comment.

2. **Am I just mad and do I need to wait before I speak?** When you are mad is not a good time to judge whether a statement will have long-lasting negative impact. Just be silent for a moment to determine if you are acting reasonably or if you are too mad to judge the damage you will invoke by your statement.

3. **Is it worth it?** There is so much long-term damage that can be caused by negative or hurtful comments that it really has to be a critically important issue to take that type of risk.

4. **Could it be said a different way?** Many times a negative or hurtful statement can be said in a positive

manner with a bit of thought. Often with that bit of thought it will also be apparent that there really was no need to make the statement at all.

While actions speak louder than words, it is also true that words can help build an understanding between two people and cement a lasting relationship. On the flip side, all too often people forget that one negative or hurtful statement can undo an entire day's positive actions and words, damaging the very core of the relationship. So, be mindful of choosing words that will enhance your relationship each and every day.

CHAPTER 3 2

Great love is best not rushed

*Accepting true love takes
courage and trust.
Giving love away takes time.*

"YOU HAVE TO WALK carefully in the beginning of love; the running across fields into your lover's arms can only come later when you're sure they won't laugh if you trip." This marvelous quote by Jonathan Carroll is from *Outside the Dog Museum.*

We think this is wonderful advice for those "falling in love." Too often, two people feel the early signs of a loving relationship only to move too fast and scare away the one they are falling in love with. Or worse yet, they become so enamored with "being in love" that they become blinded to the warning signs. They so desperately want to be in love and be loved that they miss important clues to the real feelings of the one they love.

In our many interviews over the years with individuals who have had a successful and long-term relationship with somebody, we have repeatedly heard this advice—go slow in the beginning.

You've heard the old expression, "Rome wasn't built in a day." One thing for certain—neither was love. It develops over time. It requires patience. It requires self-examination. And it most certainly requires you to run slowly across fields until you find the proper footing, lest you fall down!

Building confidence in any budding love relationship takes time and commitment. It requires a level of objectivity about what is going on at a level you may have never reached before. People falling in love do not lie to each other, but they often lie to themselves about what is happening to them. They let feelings and emotions get the best of them before they are truly ready to share their heart with another—before they are ready to make the honest and caring commitment required to make love last.

Recently, someone sent us a copy of a beautiful essay entitled "Letters To My Son" by Kent Nerburn. Our favorite passage is excerpted below:

Here "is where many lovers go wrong. Having been so long without love, they understand love only as a need. The first blush of new love is filled to overflowing, but as their love cools, they revert to seeing their love as a need. They cease to be someone who generates love and instead become someone who seeks love. They forget that the secret of love is that it is a gift, and that it can be made to grow only by freely giving it away."

The message here should be clear—love is a gift you give to someone, and if you are lucky, they give it back in return. But the real lesson here is that you need to step back and make sure that you feel good about giving your love away as a gift. And to do this takes time. It takes reflection. It requires being honest with yourself about what you are feeling and what you are giving away to another human being. Rushing to judgment about matters of such profound importance is never a wise thing to do. Giving love away takes time. Accepting true love takes courage. And trust. And time.

There are clear and telltale signs for love that you can read about in the chapter, *How will you know you are really in love?* When you recognize the seven categories for knowing you are in love, honestly reflect upon them, and cherish them as the gift of love that they are, you are in love. But don't confuse your feelings of love for another, your gift of love to another, without also truthfully asking yourself, "Have I also received the gift of love from the one I love?"

When you feel good about giving your love as a gift and that feeling is reciprocated by the one you love, then you both are in love with each other. As Nerburn tells us, the "secret of love is that it is a gift, and that it can be made to grow only by giving it away."

True and lasting love takes time because true and lasting love is all about the reciprocal gift of love between two human beings. To be in love is to dash across the field of lilies on a beautiful spring morning unafraid to fall down as you leap into the arms of the one you love and who loves you. Go, be in love with the guy you are thinking about marrying, if you are ready to give the gift of love.

Enhance your relationship by NOT communicating

The guy you want to marry really doesn't want to feel suffocated. You can demonstrate a great deal of understanding when you respect his need for privacy and aloneness.

S TOP THE PRESSES!!! We have discovered what may be the most important ingredient of a successful relationship! And you know what it is? The answer is . . . drum roll, please . . . NOT communicating, by allowing time for those who inhabit the relationship *to be alone!*

Successfully married couples throughout the world have told us this very simple truth during our interviews with them—one of the

most important secrets to their successful marriage is NOT communicating. That means having time to be all to themselves—to their
own thoughts, their own meditations, their own self, and their own
physical space.

Isn't this an interesting notion? In the best marital relationships
between a man and a woman, having time alone tops the chart of
what makes their marriage work. You can take this advice to the
bank!

We have heard this expression, or some variation of it, over and
over during our travels and interviews on the world's seven continents. The amazing consistency of the stories we have heard about
aloneness have surprised us on the one hand, but have assured us on
the other. Here's why.

This is what we have learned to be true—critical to any successful marriage is to be *content with yourself.* Only those who are
capable and willing to spend time alone can be described as content
with themselves.

If you can't live in your own skin, it is difficult to share yourself
with someone else. Being content with oneself is the pre-requisite to
engaging in a healthy, happy, and successful relationship with
another human being.

There are many lessons to be learned from this notion of *aloneness* in any successful relationship, but the most essential lessons are:

1. **The most important pre-requisite to a successful relationship with another person is being content with
   yourself.** Learn to live within your own skin. *Liking
   you comes first.* That's why the first section of this
   book is entitled *The Right You.* Liking yourself allows
   for the development of positive relationships with

others. Work on this notion as if your relationship depended on it!

2. **Respecting your own need for privacy and aloneness is an important first step in building a loving relationship with the guy you want to marry.** There is a fundamental predisposition of every human being to have time alone. Recognizing and understanding that need in yourself and the guy you love is a huge step towards building a love will last for a lifetime.

3. **Aloneness is not a bad word! Spending time alone is good for everyone.** Not recognizing this need can be highly detrimental to your relationship with the one you love. Learn this lesson well. If you never give yourself or the one you love time to be alone, you do so at the detriment of your relationship.

4. **Too many failed marriages report to us this fact with alarming consistency—their spouse would not give them time to be alone to themselves.** When we probed the meaning of all this they reported to us one important finding by saying, "My spouse suffocates me!" The meaning of suffocation in a nutshell—I had no time to my own thoughts, my own being, and my own feelings. My spouse did not respect my need nor their own, to be alone. The suffocation destroyed our marriage!

5. **We feel assured that the need to be alone is a "universal truth."** Successfully and happily married couples around the world have reported this "truth" to us repeatedly and overtly. This notion is not an American thing. It is not a European thing. It is not an Asian thing. An important secret ingredient for the

best marriages around the world is to respect the need for privacy and aloneness in yourself and in the one you love. Never forget it! All successful marriages are built on this foundation.

Give your life's partner the gift of privacy and aloneness. Practice this skill even before you get married. He really doesn't want to feel suffocated. You can demonstrate a great deal of understanding when you respect his need for privacy and aloneness. The guy you are planning to marry will love you for it.

CHAPTER 34

You cannot accept infidelity

*The bottom line is this—if you
are not sure that the guy you want
to marry will be faithful to you
and not engage in
infidelity, do NOT marry him.*

*F*RANKLY, IF WE HEAR YET
one more person talk about infidelity in a relationship as if it were
okay, not a big deal, and forgivable, we are going to get angry! The
best marriages would never engage in unfaithfulness—they would
never engage in infidelity.

Here is the whole truth about what infidelity really is. Infidelity
is being disloyal to the one you love and it is an unpardonable sin!
Why would anyone who engages in this disloyal, dishonest, and

morally reprehensible behavior think it is okay? To betray someone you purport to love is unconscionable. And as we often say, there is a "character element" to marriage and to violate the "code of conduct" in a marriage—to engage in the ultimate form of betrayal—is to destroy the core, the heart, of that relationship.

We are not angry people. Clearly, we are not unreasonable people. And the truth is, we know what makes marriages work. Being unfaithful to the one you love is not conducive to a wholesome, successful, and endearing relationship.

Here's the deal—there are NO excuses for infidelity! There is no way to excuse infidelity or for you as a woman to accept it. Being unfaithful to the one you love is the most unpardonable of all sins. When a man violates the "core of trust" in your loving relationship, he will destroy the relationship.

It is our considered opinion, based on many years of research, that the notion of character in marriage is real. To suggest otherwise is to ignore the basic tenets of successful relationships. We guess that it is time to say, "The buck stops here!" Literally translated, that means that there are no excuses for disloyalty and infidelity to the one you love.

Over the years, we have interviewed a lot of people who purported to be in love. We have interviewed a lot of couples that repeated the vows, "Until Death Do Us Part." And these are not just words! To love someone for a lifetime does not occur by accident. To be in love is not an accident. To be in love is to do the simple things day in and day out of your relationship with the one you say you love. But trust us on this—you cannot betray the one you love and expect your marriage to survive and thrive.

It pains our hearts to see couples espouse the virtues of the "Desperate Housewives," who think it's okay to cheat on the one they love, and who believe that in the end everything will be okay if they do. It seems impossible to think that there are people engaged in a loving relationship who think that betrayal is an offense for which there is forgiveness.

The ultimate betrayal of the one you say you love is for most an unrecoverable act! Counselors, psychologists, therapists, and writers who suggest otherwise are not only fooling themselves, they are misleading those they purport to represent.

Don't be fooled and don't be foolish. There is rarely EVER a recovery from a relationship that sinks to betrayal, infidelity, and disloyalty. Those who have been successfully married for years and years know this to be true. Don't be misled by those who suggest otherwise.

The bottom line is this—if you are not sure that the guy you want to marry will be faithful to you and not engage in infidelity, do not marry him. If he has shown any indications of this type of behavior while you were dating or engaged, give serious consideration to moving on without him. This is not an issue that you can equivocate about. It is definitely a deal-breaker!

ॐ

CHAPTER 35

21 ways to make your love last

*Great marriages require much work
on a daily basis to establish habits
that will lay the foundation for positive
interactions and mutual
support in your marriage.*

THE KEY INGREDIENTS THAT define a successful marriage are easy to understand, yet difficult for many couples to practice in their relationship. Here are 21 ways to help you begin building the foundation of your relationship.

1. **Be a relationship cheerleader.** Be the number one cheerleader for the guy you love. Support him in every way you can. Let your partner know just how important he is to you and to the rest of the world.

2. **Learn to compromise.** Compromise is a part of daily living in a relationship. No one can have it all his or her way. Discuss how the two of you make decisions. Establish a plan to work through important issues until you both can find a mutually agreeable solution.

3. **Share the burdens.** Carry the burdens of your relationship on four shoulders, not just two. Learn to sense when your partner needs help, even when he does not ask for it. Helpfulness should become such a matter of habit that you will feel and act like a winning team.

4. **Communicate constantly.** Couples must talk about anything and everything. In successful marriage there are no sacred cows—no secrets. The same is true of your relationship right now. Build those communication skills between the two of you early in your relationship.

5. **Leave anger outside the bedroom.** Never go to bed mad—talk it over first and settle things before sleeping. You may have one very long night before going to bed, but you will get the problem resolved. While this is the number one piece of advice from the thousands of happily married couples we have interviewed throughout the world, it is also true for your relationship right now. Don't part ways angry. Solve the problem before first!

6. **Don't be ruled by emotions.** Keep your emotions in check when discussing those "sacred cow" issues. These sensitive discussions can be contentious and often heat up quickly. Don't let your emotions inter-

fere with the importance of talking openly about everything.

7. **Make loving behavior a habit.** Successful relationships are about mutual love and respect. Habits can be formed either for good or ill, so why not make it a habit to always treat the guy you love the way you would want to be treated? Make it a pervasive characteristic of your relationship.

8. **Respect the individuality of the guy you love.** Your partner is a complex individual with many interests, ideas, desires, habits and experiences. Don't narrowly define his capabilities. Allow him to grow and enhance those individualities without feeling smothered, cornered or pushed in a different direction.

9. **Do not ever get jealous or angry with the guy you want to marry when he needs to be alone.** If he senses your displeasure, he either won't allow himself the opportunity to be alone or he will resent you for being jealous or angry because of his need to be alone. Remember, the absolute need for occasional privacy and aloneness is a fundamental predisposition of every human being.

10. **Successful couples understand that taking care of themselves in a health sense is not sufficient.** You must also promote the good health of your mate. To live until "death do us part" requires a mutual concern about good health, including taking proper medications, going to annual physicals, eating healthy, getting proper sleep and having good exercise habits. Start now to promote good health, even before the wedding.

11. **Use common sense about what you put into your body.** Eat lots of fresh fruits, vegetables and whole grains, while cutting way down on salt, refined sugar, white flour, food preservatives, coloring agents, artificial flavoring, hydrogenated fat, nicotine and alcohol.

12. **Smile and laugh together often.** Remember, it takes more muscles to frown than to smile. Save your energy—smile at your guy instead of frowning. It is the simplest of expressions with the most powerful positive effects.

13. **It is NOT your money and my money.** In successful marriage it is OUR money. Start your marriage as a one-checkbook family. Now is the time to talk about this issue before you get married. How you handle your money together will say a lot about how well you form a team with common achievable financial goals.

14. **Pay all of your bills together.** That doesn't mean both of you have to actually sit down together to pay the bills. Rather, it means that both of you need to know exactly what the bills are, what is being paid, and what are the outstanding financial commitments. Open the discussion about this with what bills each of you currently have, what debts you intend to incur before you get married, and how you are going to pay those bills once you are married.

15. **Never make a major purchase without talking it over with your spouse and then sleeping on it.** You would be surprised at the number of major purchases you don't make if you just sleep on it! This is a great issue to work on before the wedding by talking about your plans for where you will live, what car you will drive,

what you absolutely have to purchase to begin your lives together, and what purchases can wait for a while. Set a limit on the amount of debt you can incur before it requires an open conversation with the guy you are in love with. The amount of debt each of you bring into the marriage is a critical point to talk about before the wedding day.

16. **Touching each other multiple times per day is the norm in successful marriages.** Touching says, "I love you so much I simply must touch you." So make a point of touching the guy you love in some way at least ten times a day.

17. **Spend time just hugging each other.** Nothing can make you feel more attached to each other than a hug. Enjoy soaking up the warmth and security you feel when the two of you grab each other for a hug.

18. **Use touching as your Morse code to make an exclamation mark of your love.** Touch your guy as you compliment what you really like about the way he looks. This little habit forces you to pay careful attention to the best qualities of the guy you love.

19. **A successful relationship is exciting, full of unpredictable things, and never boring.** Don't always do that which is predictable. Upend expectancies. Variety is the spice of life. Bring that excitement into your relationship everyday.

20. **Make an extra effort to always look your best for the guy you love.** Happily married couples report to us during their interviews that they work hard to always look their best for the one they love. In fact, they brag

about how each other looks and the appreciation they feel for the effort they put into looking nice.

21. **Send your guy a love letter or a romantic email.** Do it when it is least expected, knocking him off his feet with surprise. Taking the time to put into words how much your guy means to you is the greatest of gifts.

These 21 tips will help you enhance the relationship with the guy you love. You will begin forming a habit of taking positive actions to build your love for a lifetime together.

None of the successful couples we have interviewed around the world have said that their relationship was always fair, just and beautiful all the time. Quite the contrary, even the best marriages have stressful and challenging times. Great marriages require much work on a daily basis to build habits of positive interactions and mutual support, but the benefits you will gain from a lifetime of successful marriage are tremendous.

12 lessons of love from a penguin

The most important lessons of all
are the lessons about love and relationships
that we learned from
the Penguins of Antarctica.

*W*E JUST RECENTLY returned from the continent of Antarctica. Oh, my, what an amazing expedition it was! As human beings, we will never be the same!

For us, it was the 7th and final continent in our journey in search of great marriages around the world. Our project has taken 31 years to complete. We have interviewed couples in all 50 states of the union, 48 foreign countries, and on all seven continents of the world.

While exploring Antarctica, we interviewed couples that live and work there, observed the wildlife, and learned a lot of valuable lessons. The most important lessons of all are the lessons about love and relationships that we learned from the Penguins of Antarctica—particularly the Gentoo, the Adelie, the Emperor, and the Chinstrap. They are all interesting to observe, to say the least.

Over the course of our observations we learned that Penguins and humans have a whole lot in common. In fact, it is clear to us that Penguins and humans share many common and pervasive characteristics when it comes to love and life.

Penguins know how to sustain a relationship with their loved one. Their actions can teach us a lot. **Here are the twelve important lessons about love and life we learned from the Penguins of Antarctica:**

1. **Look out for each other.** Like humans, penguins live in towns and villages called rookeries because it's easier to protect each other from predators and from the cold weather by residing in groups. And what's really nice—most have a short commute to work finding food!

2. **Have fun and play a lot.** Penguins, like humans, love to gather with friends and family to have fun and play. Frequently, penguins just stop and admire the view— what we humans would call, "stopping to smell the roses." They often stand together to admire the view from where they live and travel. We humans should play more and take time to smell the roses!

3. **Communicate effectively.** Penguins talk and chatter a lot to each other. Communication is at the heart of their relationships with each other, just as it is with humans.

4. **Be a responsible adult.** As they grow older, penguins learn to spread their wings, and even though they will never fly, they grow up for the most part to be responsible and productive adults. Almost all become parents at some point in their life. Sounds like a familiar human story to us.

5. **Build your support network.** Sometimes penguins take trips together with their extended family. Like us, penguins know that friends and family are an integral part of their support network.

6. **Smile a lot.** Penguins are certainly a happy lot! They rarely get discouraged and almost never give up on their goals. We humans could take a major lesson from their determination. It sometimes takes that type of determination to work through the issues of life in a relationship and make it work for a lifetime of happiness. Tough situations are made better by taking a positive approach, smiling a lot, and never giving up.

7. **Shout your love to the heavens!** Penguins shout their love for each other by screaming it to the heavens! They are not shy about expressing their love for their mate. Saying "I love you" is just a normal part of their day and they are willing to express their sentiments often. We humans could learn to do a better job of this by observing the penguins!

8. **Watch out for danger.** They almost always look left and right before crossing the path! They know the world is full of danger, but you can always count on them to be prudent and careful—for their safety and for the safety of their family and friends. Watching

out for danger, being prudent and careful are a great characteristics to have in a relationship with the one you love.

9. **Keep your body clean.** Penguins love to bath a lot, especially with each other. They will race to get to the water first. Sometimes a refreshing swim makes them jump for joy!

10. **Be faithful to the one you love.** Penguins are monogamous, often having one mate for a lifetime. Death of their life's partner is about the only circumstance that causes them to search for a new mate. Maybe younger humans should pay attention to the penguin's model!

11. **Share the parenting responsibilities.** Like humans, penguins share in the nurturing, feeding, and parenting of their children. It is remarkable how penguins demonstrate that birthing, protecting, and raising a child is a shared responsibility of both the mother and the father. You can count on them to work together to build a confortable nest for their children.

12. **Argue fairly and don't hold grudges.** Penguins squawk and often times engage in lively discussions and arguments. They get in each other's face, but they usually resolve their differences in a positive fashion. Like human couples penguins argue—there is nothing wrong about that—but they have learned to argue fairly and effectively, almost never holding grudges. You can learn a lot from a penguin.

It is clear that penguins and humans have a lot in common when it comes to marriage and relationships. They have mates—often for a lifetime—love to be around family and friends, and dearly love their children.

They may live at the end of the world, but in the end, we are all very much alike. You can learn a lot about love and relationships from the penguins of Antarctica!

THE PERFECT WEDDING!
NOW WHAT?

HOW TO MARRY THE RIGHT GUY

CHAPTER 37

Is a perfect marriage possible?

*People who have gone
through the wars of life
together will always choose
their mate in battle.*

*T*OO OFTEN, PEOPLE ASSUME
that those who have the most successful marriages live in some kind
of la-la land—a perfect world—a place where everything is fair,
just, and beautiful—a Nirvana land! Here's the truth—nothing
could be further from reality!

If there is a "most important understanding" from the thousands of interviews with successfully married couples, it is this—the
most happily married couples have experienced severe challenges to
their relationship. Some of the most successfully married couples
we have interviewed over the past 30 years have reported to us
unimaginable challenges to their marriage.

Couples have shared with us stories about the death of children, financial burdens that nearly destroyed their relationship, the horrors of losing a job, the burdens of serious health issues, the pressures of child rearing problems and the destruction caused by a transfer to another city for a work assignment that neither of them wanted, to name only a few.

These are couples that have been happily and blissfully married for a long time. These are the couples that know the secrets of a great marriage and a great relationship. The best marriages, the best relationships we have ever witnessed or interviewed—have all reported to us a litany of the great challenges to their marriages throughout their years together.

Ah, but the truth is this—the best marriages report that the challenges to their marriage ACTUALLY strengthened their marriage and their relationship. The essence of their story is, "These challenges to our relationship actually made our relationship better!"

Like all of the important lessons about love and relationships we have discovered, the most important is a simple one—challenges make you stronger. And in the end, challenges—properly dealt with together as a team—will make your relationship stronger and better.

People who have gone through the wars of life together will always choose their mate in battle. People who truly love each other will always say this to us—we are a team and we will always support each in our times of need. We can always count on each other to be there for us.

The good, the bad, and the ugly—dealing with challenges together is at the heart of the best relationships. Having another human being to rely on for support, encouragement and assistance makes life's journey sweeter.

Never assume that the best marriages live in some "Cinderella land." The best marriages have survived heart-wrenching challenges. Never minimize what the best marriages and relationships have gone through.

The challenges they have experienced have made their relationship stronger. The power of challenge to the establishment of a great relationship can be documented in the thousands of interviews we have conducted.

In the end, there is NO perfect marriage! All marriages go through tough and tumultuous times. Creating a successful marriage is not always the easiest thing to do, but if you start now the two of you can build a great marriage that will help you handle the tough times together.

CHAPTER 38

Madonna's advice about marriage

*Madonna recently gave a
newly engaged couple the
best advice possible—
never go to bed angry.*

WHILE MADONNA IS better known for her great vocal and acting skills, recently she gave some great advice to a couple who got engaged during her Amsterdam concert. Madonna's advice was, "Never go to bed angry."

Madonna just gave the newly engaged couple the best advice possible. We have heard this same advice from thousands of happily married couples on all seven continents of the world.

Towards the end of our interview protocol we ask these wonderfully successful couples if they could offer some advice that we could share with newlyweds. And guess what, the number one piece of advice these happily married couples have given, is "Never go to bed mad at each other!" It has been consistently number one for more than 30 years.

Remember, this advice comes from thousands of happily married couples in 48 countries of the world. The advice these couples gave isn't designed to shock the media with something unusual or out of the ordinary. These are the words of couples with a proven track record. Madonna had it exactly correct with her advice!

The good news about the notion of "Never go to bed made at each other," it is based on research from those who would know best—those who have been happily, blissfully, and successfully married for 30-77 years! It was delightful to hear Madonna giving a newly engaged couple exactly the right advice when many so-called "experts" routinely miss the boat!

Married couples do, from time to time, have disagreements. They argue over big things and little things. They argue over stuff that doesn't matter and stuff that does. But here is what we have learned from our research—happily married couples rarely ever go to bed without resolving their differences on an issue, be it big or small.

Many couples report to us that they have stayed up all night trying to bring closure to an issue that has divided them. They know that gaining resolution is far more important than getting a good night's sleep. And remember this, issues that are not attended to more often than not fester through the night and only appear worse in the morning.

It is good to know that Madonna, who has struggled with her relationships, has now learned the most important lesson of all—never go to be mad at each other!

15 misconceptions about marriage

*While the realities of marriage can
sound daunting, the benefits of a good
marriage far outweigh the
the difficulties and challenges
present in all marriages.*

OFTEN IN LIFE, A YOUNG woman gets swept off her feet by a dashing young man. But before you fall head-over-heals in love with the guy, you have to understand what love is and the expectations and realities associated with committing yourself to a lifelong relationship.

Too many people look for the idealized version of love. Idealized love rarely happens. You will only be disappointed if you believe "idealized love" can describe your love.

When you fall in love, it is important to understand that being in love is the easy part. The rest takes hard work. And because of this, our greatest challenge as researchers who have studied successful marriage for more than 30 years, is to convince those falling in love that the Cinderella story is only the beginning of love, not the end.

The truth is, the Cinderella version of love rarely ever happens. Somewhere along the way, someone forgot to tell those who think they are in love that life isn't always fair, just, and beautiful all the time. Sometimes, the reality of love and the "Cinderella of love" are not the same.

Misconceptions and Realities about marriage:

1. **Misconception:** "Everyday of our marriage will look like a Hollywood romance novel with glittery events and romance at every turn." **Reality:** A small percentage of your time together will actually involve romance. You will still have to take out the trash, pay the bills and clean the house.

2. **Misconception:** "We'll have SEX every night." **Reality:** Johnny Cash and June Carter said it best, "We got married in a fever, hotter than a pepper sprout. We've been talkin' about Jackson ever since the fire went out." Passion cannot compete with real life and intimacy won't happen every night.

3. **Misconception:** "We'll never fight or argue because we love each other so much." **Reality:** The most successfully married couples argue and fight at various times in their relationship. It is a healthy experience as long as you fight fair.

4. **Misconception:** "We have plenty of income, so we will live happily ever after." **Reality:** Even if you happen to be in an upper income level when you get married, there is no guarantee that your income will remain high, that both of you will keep your jobs, that you will not have to move to keep a job, or that one of you will not face serious health issues effecting your employment later on in life.

5. **Misconception:** "We have always had good luck so we will be lucky in marriage." **Reality:** Luck has very little to do with a successful marriage. Rather, a successful marriage takes hard work and commitment to make love last for a lifetime.

6. **Misconception:** "Love is all we need because our love is so passionate and strong." **Reality:** Friendship, support, respect and trust are collectively what makes for a strong love, that intensifies over a lifetime together. While passionate love is great, it is not enough to sustain a relationship over a lifetime.

7. **Misconception:** "Since I am a self-sufficient person, our marriage will be easy because I don't have to depend upon my spouse for support." **Reality:** Everyone needs someone to lean on. Being a Lone Ranger does not work in a marriage. One of the greatest benefits of being married is the support and encouragement each individual gets from their spouse.

8. **Misconception:** "We will be even closer when we have kids." **Reality:** Happily married couples report that while children are a joy they also bring stress and tension to the relationship. Nora Ephron said it best,

"Having a first child is like throwing a hand grenade into a marriage."

9. **Misconception:** "My spouse will always know what I am thinking." **Reality:** Your spouse will not know what you are thinking unless you tell him or her what you like, what you dislike, or what you want to do for fun over the weekend. When you lash out at them they will not know that you are angry about work, and not them. They will not know you love them unless you tell them! This misguided guarantee can lead to a great many disappointments.

10. **Misconception:** "Everyday will be a 'MasterCard Adventure' in some exotic place, doing exciting things." **Reality:** While that may occur from time to time, it is rarely the norm.

11. **Misconception:** "Now that we are married, we will always be happy." **Reality:** You have to find happiness within yourself before you can be happy in a marriage. A successful marriage requires both inhabitants of the marriage to be happy. It is not an either/or proposition.

12. **Misconception:** "Now that I am married I will no longer be lonely." **Reality:** Marriage can be a marvelous friendship and a lifelong relationship, but you, yourself, will have to join in to make it a friendship without loneliness. It doesn't occur by accident.

13. **Misconception:** "Now that we are married, I will get everything I want in life." **Reality:** No one in a marriage gets everything they want. A marriage is about compromise and finding satisfaction in life together.

14. **Misconception:** "If you are married for 30 or more years, you will have a happy marriage." **Reality:** Only couples who work at their relationship and achieve a satisfying relationship together will be happy. Just being married for 30 or more years does not make you happy. Love is not about longevity! True love has a higher standard.

15. **Misconception:** "There will be a Magic Genie who cleans our house." **Reality:** You and your spouse will have to divide up the routine responsibilities that are required to get things done. Marriage should be a shared relationship.

Going into marriage with your eyes wide open by knowing the difference between the misconceptions and the realities of marriage will greatly improve your chances for success. While the realities of marriage can sound daunting, the benefits of a good marriage far outweigh the difficulties and challenges that are present in all marriages.

Is marriage still the norm?

*Marriage is still among the
greatest structures for social order
that exists in the world today.*

*W*E KNOW, WE HEAR
them all the time – those purveyors of half-truths, un-truths, and
political agendas. You know the ones—the ones who continually
pronounce to the world that traditional marriage is dead. Well, all
we can say is—don't believe it!

Recent reports suggest that worldwide, each year there are
approximately five marriages for each divorce. Hardly sounds like
the death of marriage to us.

The Media, Hollywood, and the pundits on the Internet and
social media, have contributed greatly to the notion that the

"abnormal" is "normal." Our research tells us clearly that "marriage norms" still predominantly prevail, but many, including the media, try desperately to depict a different scenario. Little wonder that many people take on practices like "cohabitation," have children out of wedlock, consider traditional marriage obsolete, and promote gay marriage as the "new normal."

In a nutshell, the Normal Curve demonstrates that in a population of people, there is a "distribution around the average." Statistically, it would be fair to say that what most people consider "normal" falls within this 68% range. The farther people fall outside that range the less their behaviors and practices represent "normal" or "average."

Many folks who work with statistical data refer to the two ends of the Normal Curve as "the pinches" of the curve (think of pinching each end with your thumb and index finger). People who fall here deviate *significantly* on both ends from the majority who fall in the middle. In other words, practices or behaviors that fall in these ranges are not considered "normal."

Marriage between a man and a woman is still the norm as the solid majority (approximately 80%) of both men and women will get married at least once within their lifetime to someone of the opposite sex. *So, being a married adult IS the norm, not the exception.*

Marriage between a man and a woman has been the norm for over 3,000 years and the strongest glue of social order and the propagation of the species for the same or longer period of time. Heterosexual marriage is the norm worldwide and will continue to be so well beyond our lifetimes.

There is no disputing the fact that marriage is alive and well in the world today. So, why do the purveyors of negativism continue to distort the truth? Why do certain members of the media and so many of those who write books about the demise of marriage continue to distort the reality of what is?

There are probably lots of reasons to explain this phenomenon. Foremost among them are the polltakers. Polltakers are notorious for asking the wrong questions or asking poorly phrased questions, and then reporting results that are, well, grossly out of touch with the reality they purport to represent.

Here is an example. A recent New York Times article reported that fewer than half of American women were now married. Yet, they included in their population of "un-married women" girls who were 15, 16, and 17 years old and women whose husbands were diseased! See our point? Does anyone really believe that 15-year-old girls are "women?" Of course not! Does anyone really believe that a 70-year-old widow is "unmarried?" Of course not!

Marriage is still among the greatest structures for social order that exists in the world today. Marriage is not in danger just because a pollster asks a question that suggests it is. Marriage is not in danger just because people who report statistical data report it incorrectly or in a way that leads to a false conclusion about marriage. The truth is, marriage is alive and well worldwide AND in the United States of America.

Marriage is still the greatest and most profound commitment to love that exists, irrespective of the so-called truths exposed by pollsters who might suggest something otherwise based on faulty or distorted polling data.

When you discount for the number of divorcees in America who get divorced multiple times, the "divorce rate" and its impact is much less than that reported by the popular media. As we have said before, the "real" divorce rate in the USA in terms of its true societal impact is far less than the 50% rate so often reported. When discounted for those who have multiple divorces, the "true" impact divorce rate is probably closer to 35% or 40%.

All we ask is that the good folks who read polls and crunch numbers do so very carefully. The conclusions you draw will often be different from those concluded by the pollsters, the popular media, and the so-called experts.

Marriage is still the norm in the USA and around the world. To suggest otherwise is to ignore the real facts.

CHAPTER 41

Celebrity marriages you can model

*We have conducted an endless search
of data sources to find out the
success rates of celebrity marriages.*

*W*HO SAYS CELEBRITY
marriages don't last? We guess you might say, "They'd be wrong!"

We have conducted an endless search of data sources to find out
the success rate of celebrity marriages. And before you ask, we
excluded politicians, political pundits, and those who spin the news!
We were only interested in the success rates of famous celebrities,
particularly those who live and reside in or near Hollywood or New
York City. And the truth is, we might have missed a few. We only
hope those celebrities will let us know if we omitted them so they
can be added to this marriage honor role.

Clearly, we do not pretend to have included every successful celebrity marriage in Hollywood and New York. We only included those whose successful marriages seemed compelling and whose union would be easily recognized by the average person on the street.

Here is the list of "celebrity marriages" we came up, their wedding dates and the number of years each couple has been married:

Anne Meara and Jerry Stiller: 9/14/54 – 59 years

James Garner and Lois Clarke: 8/17/56 – 57 years

Alan and Arleen Alda: 3/15/57 – 56 years

Paula Prentiss and Richard Benjamin: 10/26/61 – 52 years

Martin Sheen and Janet Templeton: 12/23/61 – 52 years

Bill and Camille Cosby: 1/25/64 – 49 years

Christopher Walken and Georgianne Thon: 1/1969 – 45 years

Ron and Cheryl Howard: 6/7/75 – 38 years

Suzanne Somers and Alan Hamel: 11/7/77 – 36 years

Meryl Streep and Don Gummer: 9/30/78 – 35 years

Phil Donahue and Marlo Thomas: 5/21/80 – 33 years

Samuel and Latanya Jackson: 8/3/80 – 33 years (together for 43 years)

Dustin and Lisa Hoffman: 10/12/80 – 33 years

Ozzy and Sharon Osbourne: 7/4/82 – 31 years

Denzel and Pauletta Washington: 6/25/83 – 30 years

Dan Aykroyd and Donna Dixon: 4/29/83 – 30 years

Jamie Lee Curtis & Christopher Guest: 12/18/84 – 29 years

D.L. and LaDonna Hughley: 2/22/86 – 27 years

Mark Harmon and Pam Dawber: 3/21/87 – 26 years

Tom Hanks and Rita Wilson: 4/30/88 – 25 years

Kevin Bacon and Kyra Sedgwick: 9/4/88 – 25 years

Michael J. Fox and Tracy Pollan: 7/16/88 – 25 years

Kevin Kline and Phoebe Cates: 3/5/89 – 24 years

Bruce and Kris Jenner: 4/21/91 – 22 years

John Travolta and Kelly Preston: 9/12/91 – 22 years

Steven Spielberg and Kate Capshaw: 10/12/91 – 22 years

Clint Black and Lisa Hartman: 10/20/91 – 22 years

Warren Beatty and Annette Bening: 3/12/92 – 21 years

Sting of the "Police" and Trudie Styler: 8/20/92 – 21 years (together for 30 years)

Spike Lee and Tonya Lewis: 10/1993 – 20 years

David E. Kelley and Michele Pfeiffer: 11/13/93 – 20 years

Mark Consuelos and Kelly Ripa: 5/1/96 – 17 years

Antonio Banderas and Melanie Griffith: 5/14/96 – 17 years

Tim McGraw and Faith Hill: 10/6/96 – 17 years

Matthew Broderick and Sarah Jessica Parker: 5/19/97 – 16 Years

William H. Macy and Felicity Huffman: 9/6/97 – 16 years

The truth is, as long-time marriage researchers, we are growing weary of those who say, "Marriage is old-fashioned," "Marriage isn't important anymore," or "Marriage among celebrities doesn't last."

We are pleased to report that successful marriage is alive and well in Hollywood and New York City and amongst other well-known celebrities across the American continent.

Now you ask, "Why are so many celebrity marriages working?" **The seven key ingredients that define a successful marriage** are the same for these celebrity marriages as they are for the thousands of couples we have interviewed throughout the world. The ingredients are easy to understand, yet difficult for many couples to practice in their relationship.

These long lasting celebrity couples understand the seven keys:

- **Togetherness:** Two become one without losing the individual identities of each other. In successful marriage it is not you and me, *it is WE!*

- **Truthfulness:** Couples talk about anything and everything. In successful marriage there are no sacred cows and *no secrets.*

- **Respect:** Couples understand that you do unto others as you would have them do unto you. Successful love and marriage is about *mutual love and respect.*

- **Fitness:** Successfully married couples understand that taking care of only their health is not sufficient. They must also promote the health of their spouse. To live until "death do us part" requires a *mutual concern about good health.*

- **Joint Finances:** It is not YOUR money or MY money. In successful marriages, it is *OUR money.*

- **Tactile Communication:** Touching each other multiple times per day is the norm. In successful marriage touching says, *"I love you so much I simply must touch you."* Suprisingly, touch does not HAVE to include sex.

- **Surprise:** Love is characterized by the notions of variety and spice. Successful marriage is exciting, never boring, and full of unpredictable things. Don't always do that which is predictable. Upend expectancies. *Variety is the spice of life!*

Successful marriage, love, and relationships all require simple acts, simple gestures, simple conversations. Success in love and marriage depends upon an accumulation of the *doing the simple things* to form the foundation for building a love that lasts.

Marriage is a status symbol!

*It appears from the available
research that marriage is now regarded
as an indicator of
a successful personal life.*

*L*ET'S FACE IT, FROM ALL
of the available research we have reviewed about marriage and its
benefits, the one benefit that stands out most is this—more and
more people who get married are getting married "because marriage is a status symbol." As long-time marriage advocates and
researchers, we are most pleased by this recently identified benefit
of marriage.

Over the years, we have identified many benefits of marriage.
The fact of the matter is this—marriage has become an important
indicator of a successful personal life in the United States and
around the world! Marriage is the single greatest contributor to

social order on planet Earth and the most profound commitment to lasting love that exists. Those who question its importance ignore the facts.

Statistically, there is substantial support for our point of view. According to the best estimates we can find, there were nearly 45,000,000 marriages worldwide last year. There were approximately 9,000,000 divorces in the same year. If you do the math you can see that worldwide, marriages outnumber divorces by a ratio of 5 to 1. Stated clearly and succinctly, there were five marriages for every one divorce in the world last year. Hardly sounds like the death of marriage to us!

When you discount for the number of divorcees in America who get divorced multiple times, the "divorce rate" and its impact is much less than that reported by the popular media. The "real" divorce rate in the USA in terms of its true societal impact is far less than the 50% rate often reported. When discounted for those who have multiple divorces, the true "impact divorce rate" is closer to 35-40%.

In fact, the national per capita divorce rate has declined steadily since its peak in 1981 and **is now at its lowest level since 1970.** The fact that the per capita divorce has declined should be cause for celebration.

We have seen a positive trend developing and it is highly encouraging. The good news is more and more couples are committed to making their marriage work! In a society that is often characterized as "a disposable society," marriage has too many benefits to be routinely "disposed."

Interestingly, it is clear that some 75% (three-quarters) of folks who get married today met the traditional ways (work and school, friends and family, church/synagogue/place of worship). Just 20%

get married who meet through bars and social events, and from an on-line dating sites. Traditional ways of meeting a future spouse continue to dominate for those who ultimately get married.

After a lengthy review of the current research on the benefits of marriage, we have selected what we think are **the top 12 reasons marriage is the greatest contributor to social order** in the good old USA:

1. **The most powerful conclusion of all of the studies is that there is a direct positive relationship between longer life and being married.** One study concluded that men who are married live an average of 10 years longer than unmarried men and women live an average of 4 years longer than unmarried women. What an incentive to find a mate for life!

2. **There have been a great number of research studies throughout the world since 1987 demonstrating a positive relationship between being married and better physical health.** The links between marriage and good physical health are overwhelming. Married men and women have lower rates of serious illness and are less likely to die in hospitals than unmarried men or women.

3. **Married people report being happier than unmarried people.** They are hopeful, happy and feel good about themselves. A multitude of studies demonstrate the same results.

4. **Men and women in stable relationships have higher levels of psychological health.** Married people have lower rates of depression and schizophrenia than

unmarried people. They are more balanced and less likely to experience mental illness.

5. **A relationship provides a man and a woman with a built-in support system.** Research indicates that individuals in a marriage feel supported, saying that they always have someone they trust to confide in and to lean on in times of need.

6. **A married man or woman is less likely to abuse drugs or alcohol than an unmarried person.** Numerous studies indicate that married individuals are less likely than unmarried persons to engage in risky behaviors including the use of drugs or alcohol because of their feelings of responsibility.

7. **Married individuals have greater earnings than unmarried persons.** Numerous studies found that married men's earnings are significantly greater than unmarried men's earnings. The most recent studies of women's earning power demonstrate that married women earn more than unmarried women even when their husband's income is not considered part of their earnings. The vast majority of the studies take all of the various possible factors into consideration and the results still demonstrate greater earnings for married individuals than for unmarried ones.

8. **A married man will save more money than an unmarried man.** In the United States married individuals in their 50s and 60s have a net worth per person roughly twice that of other unmarried individuals.

9. **A married man or woman will have sex more often and enjoy it more.** Physically and emotionally

married couples report a greater satisfaction with sex than their unmarried counterparts. Married couples also have sexual intimacy more often than unmarried couples.

10. **If you are married, your children have a better chance to be healthier, doing better academically and having fewer emotional problems.** Children living in families with married parents are more likely to have proper health care, better nutrition and less stress to deal with at home. Children with married parents have significantly better grades, test scores and overall success in school than their counterparts raised in households with unmarried individuals.

11. **More couples in the 18-34 age range will be headed to the altar over the next couple years!** Marriages have increased some 4% since 2009 and will continue to increase through at least 2015 and probably beyond. After a downturn in marriage due to the USA economic downturn, marriage is now on the rebound, and that is good news. The biggest increases are among women ages 25-34, college-educated, and the more affluent. Marriages are declining or growing stagnant for those with a high school education or less and the poor and less affluent. The good news is this – marriage thrives among those who get married at the "right time."

12. **Drum roll please . . . number 12 is this – Marriage is now a status symbol!** It appears from the available research that marriage is now regarded as an indicator of a successful personal life. Marriage is now considered a "privileged position" in society. According to

"Hollingsworth v. Perry, marriage "confers a special validation of the relationship between two individuals and conveys a message to society that domestic partnerships or civil unions cannot match."

It is our profound belief that the value of marriage to the world will not change over the next 50 years. Marriage is here to stay.

Trust us when we say this—the numbers tell us that the marriage rate per 1000 Americans will stay about the same or increase as the USA and world economy gets better, as it always has under similar circumstances for time immemorial. Keep the faith!

CHAPTER 43

The perfect wedding! Now what?

Getting married is the easy part for most couples. Being married is when the difficult work begins.

AS A BRIDE, YOU LOOKED gorgeous in your beautiful wedding dress, the groom looked handsome and dashing, and the marriage ceremony was a fairy tale that had come true. When you tossed your bouquet of flowers into the crowd after the wedding, a mad scramble ensued to determine who the next lucky bride would be. All was well with the world.

Weddings are so much fun! The memories of such a joyous moment will linger in the minds of most who witnessed it for a lifetime. The photos of the wedding will hang on the wall of their new home, be stored in the photo albums of many, and fill up digital space in their iPhoto collection on their computer hard-drive. For the majority of those getting married, the recall of this significant moment in their lives together will occur frequently and exist in their repertoire of positive reflections "Until death do us part."

Getting married is, however, the easy part for most couples. *Being married* is when the difficult work begins. And all too often, married couples find it difficult to get beyond the wedding in their relationship with each other.

When the luster of the fairy tale starts to wear off and the difficult part of making a marriage work begins, many newly married couples flounder—they stumble—and sometimes, they fall. But you know what, this can all be prevented if you just adhere to the overarching facts about beginning marital engagement and follow the five simple first steps of marriage.

Here are the three overarching facts about beginning marital engagement:

1. **Fact number one:** Knowing what makes marriage work is simple to understand.

2. **Fact number two:** You have to just do the simple things required to make marriage work.

3. **Fact number three:** Successful marriage is an accumulation of doing the simple things day in and day out of your marriage.

We tell newly married couples to commit these three simple facts to memory and to practice from Day 1 if they expect their marriage to succeed. Successful marriage follows only after these important facts are learned.

Now, you are ready for the **five simple first steps of marriage** (more details about these steps appeared in earlier chapters):

1. **Commit yourselves after the Honeymoon is over to sit down together and share with each other what you want and expect from your marriage.** Lay it all on the table. What are your collective and individual expectations for the marriage? How does each want to be treated by your spouse? Are there housekeeping issues that need to be addressed? What are the democratic values you bring to the marriage? Do you have plans for children and if so, when? What about your individual educational plans? Where do you want to call home now and in the foreseeable future? And the list goes on. The point is, issues like these must be addressed early in the marriage and they must be addressed directly. Questions cannot usually be answered if the questions are not asked. Issues cannot be dealt with if you don't know what the issues are. And the truth is, Step 1 is the necessary first step in building a relationship of communication, give and take, truthfulness, and trust, so necessary to building a lasting love.

2. **It is important early on in a marriage to commit each other to the "core values" you want in your marriage.** For example, successfully married couples are committed to the notion that they always put their spouse first in their relationship with each other. Marriage is not a "me" experience. Marriage is a "we" experience. Putting your needs before those of your partner is not a core value either of you should commit to. Rather, putting each other first lays the foundation upon

which your new marriage can build. In addition, committing to caring and unconditional love for each other strengthens the foundation of your marriage. Being mutually responsible, trustworthy, and respectable towards each other adds to the fullness and richness of your relationship. Commitment to these core values will serve your marriage well over the years.

3. **Recognize and accept the fact that good sex is not the heart of your marriage!** This is the hardest lesson to learn after the honeymoon is over and the realities of everyday living in a marital relationship begin to take over. Sex can be a wonderful way to establish intimacy with the one you love. There is no debate about that. But on the other hand, if you set sexual expectations high on your list of things that will make your marriage fulfilling, you will quickly discover that sex alone will not make it so. Your marriage will make it for a whole bunch of reasons, but healthy sex is the only one of them. Successfully married couples report how important intimacy is to a loving marriage. They hug each other often, they kiss, they touch each other while talking, they sit cheek to cheek on the couch while having a conversation, they curl around each other when they sleep or just gaze at the stars, and yes, they have sex from time to time—when it's right for them. Keep sexual intimacy in perspective in your marriage. Commit to that notion from Day 1.

4. **Remember this important rule—actions speak louder than words!** Early in your marriage you must commit to the simple truth that you will be judged by your

actions and deeds, not by your words. When you commit to something with your words, your actions must follow. You cannot just talk about "sharing burdens"—you must actually share burdens. You cannot tell your spouse you love him or her while you treat him or her with disrespect. And, you cannot under any circumstances ignore the Golden Rule of life and of love—treat others as you would like them to treat you. In a successful marriage, you more often than not get what you give. Kindness, respect, the sharing of life's burdens, and being a person of integrity will be reciprocated in ways that will add to the richness and fullness of your marriage.

5. **And finally, all newlyweds must understand this very simple lesson—your marriage will not always be fair, just, and beautiful!** All of the best marriages have gone through tough times. All marriages have their challenges. How you build the foundation of your marriage in the early stages will go a long way towards determining whether your marriage can weather the various storms that lie ahead. Trust us on this—your marriage will be challenged along the way. One of you will lose a job. A family member will get very ill. A child might die. One of you will be transferred to another job location. There will be times when you wonder whether you can make it to the next day of your life. Your marriage will be challenged in ways you never imagined. It happens. Expect it. The good news, all of the most successful marriages have survived the ups and downs, and yours can as well.

All marriages go through seasons—much like the seasons of nature. Marriage is born in the Spring, blossoms over the Summer, grows to maturity in the Fall, and settles in over the Winter. When we find true love, most of us find it for a lifetime. Those marriages and relationships that last over time started with the simple planting of a seed. The seed was nourished over time. Love grown with tender and loving care matures into fully-grown love that can withstand the tests of time.

We have learned a lot about what makes marriages work over these past 30 years. If you heed the advice of all those successfully married couples we have interviewed across the globe you will have a good chance of making your marriage work—of making it not only survive, but thrive. You've had a perfect wedding and now you have a glimpse of what can come next if only you will commit to these simple notions.

CHAPTER 44

How do you get quality marriage advice?

If you get advice about love and marriage,
you had better be darn sure that
the advice you are listening to is coming
from a competent professional who
*meets **all** of the expert criteria.*

*W*HEN YOU WANT TO
get help, you need to find quality experts who provide practical love
and marriage advice. Lots of people purport to be "love and marriage experts." The Internet is full of those who claim to be. We, like
you, read their pontifications every day. But the truth is, most of
those who say they are, ARE NOT! Here's why.

We have found in over three decades of research about marriage
around the world that those who understand successful marriage
are those who, first and foremost, have actually experienced it.

Make no mistake about that. You cannot possibly understand the dynamics of marriage if you have never engaged in it. Not possible!

Some of the so-called "expert advice" we read on the Internet by charlatans who pretend to be "experts" is breathtaking! Let's be honest, when a twenty-something tells us about marriage, we simple must roll our eyes in disbelief regarding their audacity. What do they know? What experience over time do they have?

When a divorced person (often time a person with multiple divorces) tells their readers about successful marriage, one can only wonder, where did they get their chutzpah? Where do they get off telling others about success in marriage when they have failed at it themselves? Think about it. What do you learn about success from studying failure? Our years of research tell us—NOT MUCH!

One of our old mentors, Don Clifton, of the world-renowned Gallup Organization (may he rest in peace), once told us, "If you want to learn about success, study success. If you want to learn about failure, study failure. You don't learn much about success by studying failure and vice versa." Dr. Clifton had it right!

So, what is a love and marriage expert? Based on our years of experience and research, we believe you are a Love and Marriage Expert if you meet **ALL** of the following criteria:

1. **A love and marriage expert actually has experience at being successful in love and marriage.** That should-n't seem too surprising! Like us, if you have been successfully married for a long time (in our case nearly 47 years!), you are probably much more quali-fied as a love and marriage expert than someone who has been married for a short time, who has failed at marriage, or who has never been married at all. In

love and marriage, personal experience matters, make no mistake about that!

2. **Love and marriage experts know that studying SUC-CESSFUL love and marriage is the prerequisite to understanding both!** Those who have not done their homework in the appropriate way are not capable or authorized to pass judgment on the truth about love and marriage. Those who tell you about success when all they have done is study failure are not legitimate advocates for successful love and marriage. Don't be fooled or mislead by their pronouncements.

3. **Love and marriage experts have training and experience commensurate with the advice they give to others about love and marriage.** Let's be candid and straightforward about this—*being an expert has little to do with wanting to be one.* People who are love and marriage experts have training and experience commensurate with the advice they give. In other words, if an advice giver has graduate training at a reputable university in the fields of counseling, psychology, or social work, they are likely qualified to be a love and marriage expert.

4. **Love and marriage experts have a standing in the community of scholars and amongst professional practitioners.** They do NOT hang out a shingle because they feel so inclined. They offer advice because they are qualified to do so. In our case, we have years of graduate level training in counseling through an accredited university program in counseling psychology and, in Charley's case, years of experience as a faculty member in accredited and

well-respected graduate programs. People who have no formal training in the field of love and marriage have no formal standing in the "community of scholars." Those who claim to be a "life coach" without the requisite training are not qualified as love and marriage experts.

5. **Love and marriage experts who are worth their salt do research so they understand what they report and so they have first-hand data to further their understanding as love and marriage experts.** Love and marriage experts who are not active researchers and scholars/writers, are not qualified to offer advice as love and marriage experts. It's as simple as that. You cannot pretend to be an expert; you have to prove it through your credentials, experience, research and your scholarly writing.

The truth of the matter is this—if you go on-line to get advice about love and marriage, if you read books about these subjects, if you seek out a competent professional to help with your marriage or relationship with someone, you had better be darn sure that the advice you are listening to is coming from a competent professional who meets **all** of the aforementioned criteria. Don't listen to their advice if they do not.

It really is that simple.

℘

Appendix

APPENDIX A

ANSWERS TO MARRY THE RIGHT GUY QUIZ

APPENDIX B

GETTING TO REALLY KNOW EACH OTHER EXERCISE

APPENDIX C

SALAD RECIPES TO START YOUR HEALTHY LIFESTYLE

APPENDIX A

ANSWERS TO THE
MARRY THE RIGHT GUY QUIZ ©

The answers to the Marry the Right Guy Quiz are based upon more than 30 years of research with successful couples throughout the world.

1. F	12. F	23. F
2. T	13. F	24. F
3. T	14. F	25. F
4. F	15. T	26. T
5. T	16. F	27. T
6. T	17. T	28. F
7. F	18. F	29. T
8. F	19. F	30. F
9. T	20. T	31. F
10. T	21. F	32. T
11. F	22. T	33. T

You get three (3) points for each correct answer you recorded. In order to pass this test your total score must equal at least 90 points for you to be secure in the fact that you are well on your way to having a successful marriage.

Congratulations, if you scored 90 points or above. You can read this book to find ways you can reinforce and enhance your relationship. There are lots of great tips that you will relate well to, since you have a solid foundation for a great marriage.

If you scored between 70 and 90 points, you need to read this book so you and your guy can openly discuss the red flag issues (the questions you answered incorrectly) that can potentially derail the success of your long-term relationship.

If you scored below 70 points, you need to strongly reconsider the relationship you are in. There are simply too many negative indicators to predict a successful and long-lasting marital relationship. You need to read this book to learn what the right guy really looks like and what factors that need to be present to build a love that lasts.

APPENDIX B

GETTING TO REALLY KNOW EACH OTHER EXERCISE A SIX-WEEK PROGRAM

Getting to really know each other is a critical first step in building a love that will last for a lifetime together. It takes a genuine commitment to honesty, openness and sincerity when the two of you discuss these issues and questions.

The series of open-ended statements in this six-week program are intended to help you examine the relationship you have with the guy you love and to practice new methods of interacting in conversation. One of the underlying assumptions of this exercise is that periodic sharing of information with each other is good for your relationship and serves as a periodic renewal stimulator. It is also a way to take time out from everyday living to look at yourself, the guy you love, the strength of your relationship, where it is now, and where it is going.

We suggest that the two of you set aside at least thirty minutes per week for sharing your responses to each group of open-ended statements. After the six weeks, you can begin the process over again or you may wish to generate a list of topics of your own choosing and respond to those that interest you the most (careers, money, family, sex, etc.). Remember, the most important thing is that you develop the habit of routinely sharing with each other in an honest, open and sincere manner. The topics do not really matter—the conversation is what matters.

Sharing Starters

INSTRUCTIONS: For each starter, think about how you would like to complete the sentence and what additional information is needed to help the guy you love understand your thinking about the issue. Alternate turns completing the statement so each one of you will have the opportunity to begin with a fresh idea. Add as much as you can think of about each of the sharing starters. Remember, real sharing can only occur in a non-judgmental atmosphere of acceptance. There are no right or wrong answers to these open ended questions.

WEEK *1*

1. When we first met was …

2. Our relationship is best described as …

3. If we could model another couple's relationship it …

4. One way that we are alike is …

5. One way that we are different is …

6. My favorite place that I want to share with you is …

7. I see my friends fitting into our relationship by …

8. I find your friends to be …

9. When we meet new people, I …

10. When I am with you in a social situation, I feel …

11. One of the best things we ever did together was …

12. The needs you satisfy in me are …

13. I am most proud of you when …

14. When I am with you and your family I feel …

15. The amount of time I need to spend alone is …

WEEK *2*

16. The thing I enjoy most about you is …

17. One of my needs that is not yet satisfied is …

18. Something I have learned about myself is ...

19. Sometimes I have trouble when we are together dealing with ...

20. The way I deal with troublesome feelings now is ...

21. I feel indecisive when ...

22. I assume you know that ...

23. If I could make you over, I would never change ...

24. You help me the most when ...

25. I am afraid ...

26. I like it when you ...

27. You annoy me when you ...

28. One thing I regret having done is . . .

29. A habit of mine that bothers me most is . . .

30. Your greatest strength is . . .

WEEK 3

31. I have the most fun with you when ...

32. Something I would like to talk about but we seldom do is ...

33. It makes me feel very uncomfortable when you ...

34. If I had all the money in the world, I would ...

35. A frequent fantasy I have about you is ...

36. When we have an intellectual discussion ...

37. You tend to talk a lot about ...

38. When I don't want to answer questions, I ...

39. When I have trouble expressing something to you, I ...

40. One thing that is helping us to grow closer is ...

41. The activities I most like to do with you are ...

42. I tend not to tell you about ...

43. I would like to feel more equal to you when ...

44. Something I have always wondered about is ...

45. I think you avoid me when ...

WEEK 4

46. Something I am usually reluctant to discuss is ...

47. I am most proud of myself when ...

48. When I hurt you, I ...

49. To keep from being hurt, I ...

50. It hurts me when ...

51. I need you most when ...

52. I get discouraged or frustrated when ...

53. I think you are unfair with me when you ...

54. When you are pouting, I feel ...

55. The things that hold us together are ...

56. Right now I am feeling ...

57. I become most defensive when you ...

58. If I wanted to make you laugh, I would ...

59. When we fight ...

60. An important thing or issue that is between us right now is ...

WEEK 5

61. If I wanted to make you laugh, I would . . .

62. I think that you do not give me a chance to . . .

63. When I feel as if I have lost, I . . .

64. I find that being open with you is . . .

65. What I like best about our relationship is . . .

66. I wish you would let me know when I . . .

67. A pattern I see in our relationship is . . .

68. The part of my body that I like least is . . .

69. What I like most about your body is . . .

70. The ways I like you to touch me are . . .

71. What makes you most attractive to me is . . .

72. One of the times that bothered me most in our relationship was . . .

73. I feel jealous when . . .

74. The main reason I love you is . . .

75. I would like our relationship to become more . . .

WEEK 6

76. Money issues are important when . . .

77. Our financial views are . . .

78. The time I worry most about money is . . .

79. Your career makes me . . .

80. My career makes me . . .

81. My continued education is . . .

82. Your achieving success is . . .

83. Children are . . .

84. Sex to me is . . .

85. If we could live anywhere, I would like to live . . .

86. If we could be doing anything, I would most like us to . . .

87. The most exciting thing about our future is . . .

88. The thing I value most in life is . . .

89. I believe in and am committed to . . .

90. In five years, I see us . . .

APPENDIX C

SALAD RECIPES TO START YOUR HEALTHY LIFESTYLE

Collected from couples around the world

Just as the ingredients that make-up a successful loving relationship are balanced and blended together, so to are the ingredients in a healthy and delicious salad. Too much of one ingredient or not enough of another can spoil the balance and flavor of a great tasting salad.

Here are fourteen uniquely balanced salads shared with us by happily married couples we have interviewed around the world. Including generous portions of fruits and vegetables in your diet each day will enhance your communications and also improve the overall health of you and the guy you love.

From these fourteen recipes discover your favorite recipe or use variations of them to start your own set of uniquely balanced salad recipes. Each of these recipes are made with fresh ingredients and sized generously just for the two of you. Bon Appetit!

Mediterranean Salad with Tuna

We learned this recipe from a marvelous couple we interviewed in Lyon, France. They have taken the traditional Nicoise Salad recipe and added selected fresh vegetables from the gardens of Southern France.

Prepare two dishes with a bed of baby spring mixed greens. Divide the following ingredients in half and add to the top of each dish of greens:

1 stalk of celery - thinly slice

½ thin slice of red onion - chopped into small pieces

2 small red potatoes boiled, cooled and sliced into 1/8" thin slices

1 hard boiled egg, cooled and thinly slice

12 pitted Kalamata black olives

2 baby cucumbers sliced into 1/8 thick slices

6 sweet yellow cherry tomatoes cut in half

6 red cherry tomatoes cut in half

2 pieces of tuna 4" x 4" about 5/8" thick (rub with a seafood seasoning, grill, cool, squeeze lemon juice lightly over tuna.) Thinly slice and place evenly over salads.

Recommended dressing:
Squeeze fresh lemon juice lightly over salad.
Add Balsamic Vinaigrette salad dressing to taste and toss.

New Zealand Salad

During our latest trip to New Zealand, we were fortunate to interview a delightful couple happily married for 47 years. They gave us what may very well be the best salad recipe we have discovered during our interviews around the world. We hope you will enjoy it as much as we do.

Prepare two dishes with a bed of half baby field greens and half Romaine lettuce cut up into 1" pieces. Divide the following ingredients in half and add to the top of each dish of greens:

2 Tablespoons almonds thinly sliced

2 Tablespoons dried cranberries

1 Tablespoon golden raisins

1 thin slice of Portabella mushroom - Cut into 1/2" pieces

2 Tablespoons of wontons

1 Tablespoons blue cheese crumbles

2 strips of lean applewood smoked bacon - Cook and cut off fat. Crumble meat portions over salad.

Recommended dressing:
Citrus White Vinaigrette Dressing - The dressing is made by combining 2 Tablespoons of your favorite White Vinaigrette dressing and 1 Tablespoon of fresh squeezed citrus juice (mostly orange juice with few drops of lime or lemon juice).

Chicken Salad from Antarctica

Once in awhile you meet extraordinary people! Jerry and Elena Marty are two such people. And life together over their 41 years of marriage has been anything but ordinary. You see, Jerry and Elena, these two lovebirds, have actually lived and worked in Antarctica. Jerry was in charge of building the new South Pole Station, which took 15 years to complete. Elena did many jobs including driving a forklift. Here is their favorite salad, including their special dressing.

1 head of iceberg lettuce – shredded

3-6 thinly sliced green onions (use whites and some green)

¼ cup toasted sesame seeds

4 oz. package of slivered almonds toasted

½ package of rice sticks (Maifun or Saifun) - Deep fry vegetable oil in batches so that noodles puff up but stay white. Drain on paper towel to remove oil.

3 boneless chicken breasts - Cook in water with sliced fresh ginger for 20 minutes, until done. Drain, cool, shred into little pieces.

Special Dressing: 4 Tablespoons granulated white sugar

2-3 teaspoons salt

½ teaspoons black pepper

4 Tablespoons vinegar

½ cup salad oil

Heat vinegar with sugar, salt and black pepper over low heat. Dissolve sugar then let cool (put in refrigerator). Add oil after cooling. Toss on dressing at the last minute.

Jerry and Elena recommends serving as a light luncheon dish with fresh French bread/rolls and your favorite Chardonnay

----

Key West Mango Salad

While in Key West, a remarkable couple married for 32 years gave us their favorite salad recipe using fresh mangos. They liked to use Champagne mangos, but indicated that any mango will work fine as long as it has been properly ripened.

Prepare two dishes with a bed of baby mixed greens. Divide the following ingredients in half and place them artfully on the salads:

1/3 cup hearts of palm thinly sliced

2 Tablespoons toasted almonds sliced

1/3 cup sweet ripened mango diced into ¼" pieces

1 grilled slice of red onion (can be cooked in microwave with butter until lightly browned)

Recommended dressing:

Blend 1/3 cup of ripened mango with 1/3 cup of your favorite balsamic vinaigrette salad dressing. Drizzle over salad.

Alaskan Salmon Salad

As you can probably guess, this recipe comes to us from a marvelous couple living in the Alaskan Kenai area where the red salmon is famous for its quality. During their 38 years together they have used salmon in every imaginable way, but this simple recipe is their very favorite.

Prepare two salad dishes with a bed of half field greens and half chopped romaine. Top with:

Thinly sliced red onion strips (two slices quartered)

1/2 cup of blanched French green beans

1/2 cup of roasted red peppers thinly sliced

Grilled red salmon filet (serve on top whole or broken into pieces)

Recommended Dressing:

Lemon Vinaigrette or Balsamic Vinaigrette

Spanish Catalan Salad

Eating healthy is one of the seven secrets of a successful marriage. During our trip last fall to interview couples in Barcelona, Spain, we discovered this recipe. It was given to us by a marvelous couple who have been married for 39 years and enjoy focusing on salads using only the freshest of ingredients.

Prepare two dishes with a bed of 1/2 baby field greens and 1/2 Romaine lettuce pieces. Divide the following ingredients in half and add to the top of each dish of greens:

3 large green Spanish olives (pitted not stuffed) - sliced

2 Tablespoons crumbled blue cheese from a chuck of blue cheese

2 Teaspoons green onions chopped

2 pieces applewood or cherrywood smoked bacon
cooked and chopped

2 slices of beefsteak tomato diced into ¼" pieces

Recommended dressing:

Drizzle lightly with White Balsamic Vinaigrette

Irish Country Salad

On the Emerald Green Island of Ireland, they have mastered the art of growing lovely vegetables and putting them together artfully as salads. One of our favorite salads from our recent trip was the Irish Country Salad we enjoyed near beautiful lakes of Glendalough.

Make a bed of baby bib lettuce leaves. Arrange the following ingredients on the bib lettuce leaves:

Quarter a medium garden tomato

One garden fresh cucumber sliced

One radish sliced

Four slices of scallion

Four whole baby beets sliced

Boiled medium white potato ~ cooled and sliced

Accent with watercress

Recommended dressing:

Creamy mustard dressing

Grand Parisian Salad

During our recent interviews in Paris, France, a delightful couple married for 31 years gave us their favorite salad recipe to share with you. What makes this salad so special is the use of haricot verts-slender, long green beans so popular in the French cuisine.

Make two salad beds of 1/3 Romaine lettuce, 1/3 field greens and 1/3 baby spinach. Add to each salad the following ingredients:

8 baby haricot verts (small slender, long green beans)
slightly blanched

1 Tablespoon of Gorgonzola crumbles

6-8 tiny yellow cherry tomatoes

½ cup of pulled chunks of slow roasted or grilled chicken

Recommended dressing:

Drizzle with White Balsamic Vinaigrette and toss to
uniformly distribute the dressing.

The Beijing Chopped Salad

The Beijing Chopped Salad was created by a happily married couple we interviewed in China two years ago. They have been married for 52 years. We think you will agree with us that this is a wonderfully healthy salad that tastes great.

Saute one or two skinless chicken breasts until completely cooked, then add sesame peanut sauce. Set aside and cool. Mix the following ingredients in a bowl:

8 snow peas cut into ½" pieces

1/2 bell pepper cut into narrow strips ½" long

1/3 cup red cabbage cut into narrow strips ½" inch long

1/3 cup carrots Julienne cut

1/3 cup Chinese cabbage cut into narrow strips ½" long

1/4 cup of peanuts (can use almonds if peanut allergies exist)

Recommended dressing:

Put ginger honey mustard dressing on ingredients and mix. Divide into two salads and place in bowls. Add to the top of each salad 1/2 of cooled chicken and a few wonton strips.

Australian Passion Salad

This salad is the creation of an Australian couple happily married for 39 years. Blending their favorite ingredients from delicate berries to wonderfully tangy goat cheese, they produced a uniquely flavorful salad with lots of healthy fruit.

Make a bed of baby field greens on each of two salad bowls/plates. Top each salad with:

1 large strawberry cut into six pieces

5 raspberries

10 blueberries

1 Tablespoon dried cranberries

1/8 cup of pomegranate seeds

1 Tablespoon of caramelized walnuts or glazed pecan halves

Place a rounded Tablespoon of goat cheese in the center of the salad.

Recommended dressing:

Your favorite Poppyseed Dressing or Berry Vinaigrette - drizzle lightly over salad.

Buenos Aires Special Ensalada

Three things the people of Argentina love are Malbec, grilled tenderloin steak (they call it Lomo) and mixed salads. Many take pride in growing their vegetables and using them in a wide variety of salad combinations.

This particular salad recipe was given to us from a couple we interviewed in Buenos Aires on our way to Antarctica who have been married for 31 years. They grow their own lettuces and other vegetables in their rooftop garden. By adding the steak to the salad, it became the main entrée of their Sunday evening dinner.

Prepare two dishes with a bed of 3/4 baby butter lettuce and 1/4 radicchio lettuce. Next, accent the salad around the edges with Belgium endive lettuce. Divide the following ingredients in half and add to the top of each dish of greens:

12-16 red cherry tomatoes

8 small mozzarella balls (3/4" diameter)

4-5 inch baby cucumber sliced into ¼" slices (cut in half) and evenly distributed on the bed of lettuce.

3-4 thin slices (3/4" x 2") of your favorite grilled steak - Tenderloin (Lomo) works best.

Recommended dressing:

Blend 2 tablespoons of White Balsamic Vinaigrette dressing and 1/2 teaspoon horseradish sauce ~ lightly drizzle over salads.

This salad includes all of the Buenos Aires food groups - mixed salad and Lomo, accompanied by a great Malbec wine!

Tangiers Salad

Tangiers, Morocco has a rich European heritage, so it was no surprise to learn a great French salad recipe from one of the couples we interviewed there. This is a light version of the famous Salad Nicoise made by a couple who loves French cooking, but who tried to reduce the calories while still keeping the flavor in.

To make a salad for two, combine the following ingredients with 8 cups of mixed field greens:

1 medium red potato boiled but crisp and cut into quarters

4 asparagus steamed but crisp and cut into 2" pieces

1 small tomato diced into ¼" cubes

8 Kalamata olives pitted

2 anchovies

1 tuna steak (4oz.) grilled with seafood spice to taste
and cut into 1/4" thick slices

Recommended Dressing:

Lemon Balsamic Vinaigrette ** If you cannot find lemon vinaigrette, squeeze the juice from 1/2 lemon into approximately 3 tablespoons of your favorite balsamic vinaigrette.

Place all ingredients in a bowl with salad dressing and toss. This salad has a very light dressing to allow the flavors of the salad to come through. Enjoy this healthy alternative to the traditional Salad Nicoise.

Santiago Harvest Salad

When the fall winds blow and the apples are at their peak in the orchards near Santiago, Chile, Janie and Hector take great delight in mixing apples into their salads. They enjoy making this salad often, especially when they are enjoying a lovely fall afternoon along the beautiful west coast of Chile.

Make a bed of romaine cut into 1" strips and field greens on each of two salad bowls/plates. Top salads with:

1 granny apple cut into Julianne slices 1/8" thick

1 Tablespoon of golden raisins

1 Tablespoon dried cranberries

2 Tablespoons of caramelized pecans

1 thin slice red onion - Separate rings and place on salads.

2 Tablespoons crumbed feta cheese

Recommended dressing:

White Balsamic Vinaigrette

Caribbean Salad

This salad comes to you from a special happily married couple in the Yucatan Peninsula of Mexico who love combining fresh fruit with the traditional salad. When you taste this delightful unique salad, you can see why it is served often in Mexico. Hopefully it will make you think of the warm sunny Caribbean during cold winter days.

On two salad plates make a bed of Romaine lettuce – 1" pieces. Mix the following ingredients and place over Romaine lettuce:

1/3 cup fresh pineapple cut into ¼" pieces

1/3 cup fresh red papaya cut into ¼" pieces

1/3 cup fresh yellow honeydew melon cut into ¼" pieces

1/8 cup jicama diced

2/3 cup small boiled and peeled shrimp

Squeeze small amount of fresh lime juice over salad

Recommended Dressings:

Citrus Balsamic Vinaigrette

Louie, Our Lover Boy

MARRY THE RIGHT GUY

My Reflections
on Love and Marriage

_____

_____

_____

_____

_____

_____

_____

_____

_____

_____

_____

_____

_____

_____

_____

_____

_____

_____

_____

_____

_____

_____

_____

_____